Praise for Giora Romm's *Solitary*

"Fighter pilots tell the greatest stories and the great ones tell the best stories of all. *Solitary* becomes a book of meditation and the deepest philosophy when Giora Romm is shot down and captured in Egyptian territory. Romm was the first ace produced by the Israeli Air Force, a group my father considered the best pilots in the world…after those of the United States Marine Corps of course. My father was *The Great Santini* and had strong opinions on such matters. Romm's experiences as a Prisoner of War are stirring and his captivity will become legendary in POW circles. A great addition to any library dedicated to the art of war or the ability to retain one's humanity in the most inhuman circumstances."

–**Pat Conroy,** bestselling author of
The Death of Santini: The Story of a Father and his Son

"Giora Romm's *Solitary* seized me from the opening paragraph. Yes, the storytelling is spellbinding, but it is Romm's explication of the theme of the fall, ordeal and self-resurrection that places this book not only among the finest war writing ever but, like Viktor Frankl's *Man's Search for Meaning*, alongside the most profound reflections on the resilience and capacity of the human soul."

—**Steven Pressfield,** bestselling author of *Gates of Fire* and *The War of Art*

"One afternoon, before dinner, Israeli ace fighter pilot Giora Romm fell from the heaven-like sanctuary of his Mirage cockpit to the hell of ejection into Egypt, capture, captivity, torture, and unimaginable pain. Forty some years later he has given us a pitch perfect recollection of his ordeal, beautifully written, wildly challenging, a masterpiece of men at war. A story of survival, it's proof, needed today more than ever, that no matter the pit or prison, the human spirit can endure. I anxiously await the day my own sons are old enough to read it."

—**Rich Cohen,** bestselling author of *Tough Jews* and *The Avengers*

"A magnificent triumph of the human spirit. *Solitary* is a truly rare, firsthand glimpse into the hellish life and psyche of an elite warrior turned Prisoner of War. I was captivated from the first page to the last."

—**Sean Parnell,** bestselling author of *Outlaw Platoon*

"September 1969: Israeli fighter ace Captain Giora Romm is shot down over Egypt. Grievously injured during ejection and captured, he spends three months as a prisoner of war, where he is subjected to intense interrogations, vicious beatings, hunger, and long, frightening periods of solitary confinement. Released at last, he undergoes numerous surgeries and lengthy rehabilitation, during which Romm is determined to recover and rejoin his fighter squadron. *Solitary* is a gutsy story of one man's survival, endurance, and strength of will as Romm overcomes all odds to once again pilot a jet fighter in combat."

–**Larry Alexander,** bestselling co-author of *A Higher Call*

"How many books have you started reading at night, and then couldn't stop until you were done—only to look up and realize it was 4am? For me, it's only been a small handful— but *Solitary* is now on that list. This book is simultaneously heartbreaking and encouraging, incredibly cringe-worthy and compelling, and both depressing and inspiring. It grabs you immediately and doesn't let go until you're finished."

–**Tucker Max,** bestselling author of
I Hope They Serve Beer in Hell

"When an Israeli fighter ace is shot down and taken captive by Egyptian forces, he must—through his wits and will— conceal his identity, his knowledge and his fears under intense interrogation, pressure and endless solitary confinement. You will tear through this book as you accompany him on this journey from the air to a prison cell and ultimately back to the skies. It reads like fiction but is ultimately a testament to the deep power that some people have within themselves that only the worst of situations can summon and display."

–**Ryan Holliday,** bestselling author of
The Obstacle is the Way

"Even in his darkest hours, Giora Romm manages to demonstrate Admiral James Stockdale's philosophical endurance and Chuck Yeager's colorful charm. An extraordinary and powerful story of a pilot's courage enduring captivity."

–David J. Danelo, bestselling author of *Blood Stripes*

"*Solitary* is the story of one man who knows exactly what he is—warrior, guardian, patriot, ace fighter pilot—and his battle against tremendous adversity, internal and external, to remain true to his calling. Faced with crippling injuries, isolation, abuse, and fear and resistance beyond measure, Giora Romm could have given up. *Solitary* is about what he did instead. Warriors, artists, parents—those who are all three and more—this story will resonate with you."

–Jeremy Brown, author of
Find>Fix>Finish and *Show No Teeth*

"*Solitary* is a jet fueled mission of the human spirit. With equal parts *Darkness At Noon* and *Top Gun*, Israeli ace Giora Romm provides an astounding and personal journey onto the fields of battle... as a pilot, prisoner, and human being. With you as his co-pilot, he discovers that the real enemies, life's most dark and powerful opponents, are fear, loneliness and the inner me, and the best counterweights for victory... what we can arm ourselves with daily to conquer the most challenging obstacles life brings... are courage, self-control, calm and confidence.

–Chris Cavallerano, Founder, Motivo Inc.

SOLITARY

GIORA ROMM

SOLITARY

The Crash, Captivity and Comeback
of an Ace Fighter Pilot

GIORA ROMM

Translated from the Hebrew
by Anne Hartstein Pace

Black Irish Entertainment LLC

NEW YORK   **LOS ANGELES**

BLACK IRISH ENTERTAINMENT LLC
ANSONIA STATION
POST OFFICE BOX 237203
NEW YORK, NY 10023-7203

COPYRIGHT © 2014 GIORA ROMM
TRANSLATED FROM THE HEBREW BY ANNE HARTSTEIN PACE
COVER DESIGN BY DERICK TSAI, MAGNUS REX
EDITED BY SHAWN COYNE

FIRST BLACK IRISH ENTERTAINMENT
HARDCOVER EDITION JUNE 2014

SOLITARY DERIVES FROM GIORA ROMM'S ORIGINAL HEBREW
EDITION, TZIVONY ARBA (TULIP FOUR), MISKAL-YEDIOTH
AHRONOTH BOOKS & CHEMED BOOKS: TEL-AVIV, ISRAEL, 2008,
WHICH WON THE 2009 YITZHAK SADEH PRIZE FOR MILITARY
LITERATURE.

FOR INFORMATION ABOUT SPECIAL DISCOUNTS
FOR BULK PURCHASES,
PLEASE VISIT WWW.BLACKIRISHBOOKS.COM

ISBN: 978-1-936891-28-3
EBOOK ISBN: 978-1-936891-22-1

PRINTED IN THE UNITED STATES OF AMERICA

1   2   3   4   5   6   7   8   9   10

To all POWs
To all those with whom I served
To those I commanded and fought side by side with
To my wife and children, who went with me
almost everywhere

Table of Contents

INTRODUCTION

The book you're holding has been, in its original Hebrew, a best-seller and a sensation in Israel. This is its first translation into English. I believe it will take its place not only as a classic in the literature of war but as literature, period.

Giora Romm was the Israeli Air Force's first fighter ace. As a twenty-two-year-old lieutenant, he shot down five MiGs during the Six Day War of 1967.

Fourteen months later over the Nile Delta, an Egyptian missile exploded beneath the tail of his Mirage IIIC. Within moments Romm found himself hanging by the straps of his parachute, with a broken arm and a leg shattered in a dozen places, looking down from 10,000 feet. Streams of farmers and field workers converged below onto the spot toward which his chute was descending, with the intention, he was certain, of hacking him to death as soon as his feet touched the earth.

No other Israeli pilot had survived capture in Egypt or in any other Arab state.

Solitary is Romm's story of his imprisonment, torture, interrogation, release, and return to service.

Solitary is not a "war book." It's not a tale of heroism, though if anyone ever qualified for that distinction, it is this story's author. *Solitary* is not even, in its deepest parts, about captivity or imprisonment.

Solitary is about Romm's inner war.

It's the story, in his phrase, "of a fall from a great height," not only literally but metaphorically.

Romm could not tell his captors the truth about who he was or what he had done. He had to invent an entire fictional biography and keep it straight in his head through months of beatings and interrogations, all the while being held in solitary confinement with his body sheathed from chest to toe in a plaster cast.

In all the world, there is no lower place to which one can fall than the cold concrete floor of solitary confinement. And on all the planet there is no place more remote than an enemy prison cell in wartime.

But Romm's fall from a great height is only the prelude. In the deepest sense, *Solitary* does not begin until after he is repatriated to Israel, with a thirteen-inch steel rod in one thigh and an opposite arm he cannot raise high enough to set his helmet on his head or to lower the canopy of the fighter plane he returns to, not as a solitary gladiator but as a squadron commander, responsible for the lives of two dozen fliers in wartime.

To whom can Romm confide? Who can help him? Who will understand the demons raging inside his skull? Not his commanders, not his fellow pilots, not even his wife and family. Romm must fight that inner war alone in a cockpit above the same delta fields from which he first plunged to earth.

His state has become more solitary now than it was in the darkest hours of captivity.

Solitary is not a grim book. It's full of wry humor, keen self-observations and revelations.

An ordeal such as Romm endured is a sojourn in hell, but it is also a passage. Romm fell, and he came back. *Solitary* is his indelible account of confronting, as few of us ever will, his own fears and limitations, and discovering, ultimately, his capacity to survive and to prevail.

Steven Pressfield
Los Angeles
2014

One

11-SEP-1969

I am dangling beneath my parachute. Gazing down from a height of 10,000 feet, knowing I am going to be killed in less than fifteen minutes, I feel great sorrow for myself. None of my fellow pilots who've parachuted into the Nile Delta have survived the encounter with the welcoming committee below, and I have no reason to think my fate will be any different.

Moments before, I was in the cockpit of my Mirage jet, piercing the sky faster than the speed of sound, about two hundred miles from home. When a missile exploded under the tail of my plane, I tried to take control of the situation. But to no avail. There are three separate hydraulic flight systems in the Mirage, and in less than ten seconds I lost pressure in all three. When the pressure falls below 90 HPZ, the third system, the emergency system, activates a warning siren. The sound that wailed in my ears was one that can instantly cause any pilot to lose his own hydraulic pressure.

I shifted the stick, hoping to turn the plane towards home, but got no response. The feeling was like driving a child's toy car—you briskly turn the wheel from side to side, but the car careens all over the place with no relation whatsoever to the steering motion. It didn't take a big genius to understand that the time had come to give my ejection seat its moment of glory. I took one last quick glance around, raised both hands to the upper ejection handle, and pulled it hard so that it came down to chest level and peeled back the canvas that is there to protect the pilot's face. Nothing happened. I released the handle and pulled it down again, harder this time. Still nothing. I removed the canvas covering from my face and saw that I was plunging vertically towards the ground at a tremendous speed, little time left before I carved a huge crater in the earth and turned to a pile of dust to be scattered by the wind. My right hand immediately moved to the lower ejection ring, the one between the pilot's legs, and yanked it hard. The cockpit canopy flew off and I knew that in just one second the ejection process would begin. I remember thinking, *Hey, wait, there's no turning back here...* and then the storm blew up in my face.

Like a shell shot from a cannon, I passed in a flash from the quiet of the cockpit to the outside world, my body slicing through the sound barrier to wherever the supersonic, six-hundred-mile-per-hour wind would carry it.

With the Mirage, the ejection process takes 1.75 seconds to slow the pilot from the speed at which he ejected to freefall speed. When the ejection takes place at an altitude of 14,000 feet or higher—I was at 20,000 feet at the time—the pilot's parachute does not deploy. Instead, a small stabilization chute opens above the ejection seat. As the pilot falls at that altitude, he remains belted into the seat. The idea is to bring the pilot as quickly as possible, and in the most stable manner possible, to an altitude where the temperature and oxygen level are suited to human survival.

It was an utterly stunning one and three-quarter seconds. The wind pummeled me, spun my seat wildly around its three axes, and ripped off my helmet (the one with the dragon painting on it), my oxygen mask and my gloves. Then came the soft blow when the stabilization chute opened. I found myself sitting in my seat like one would wait outside a doctor's office. Only I was plummeting straight towards the ground.

My head slumped on my chest. The brutal last couple of seconds had practically knocked me senseless. But the wind blowing gently on my face soon brought me to. I opened my eyes and slowly started to look around. I looked up to confirm that the parachute was indeed holding the seat in which I sat, then looked around again and then down. Wherever I looked, it was a very strange sight. Far below me, Egypt stretched as far as the eye could see.

But right below me, I saw just one leg, my left leg. My eyes kept searching for the right leg but no, only the left was there. I started wiggling my toes and felt not only the toes of the left foot moving, but also those of the right, of my missing leg. The only place I hadn't yet looked was behind the seat, so I grasped the cord of the stabilization parachute with my right hand and turned my head as far as I could. And there was the leg—pointing in the opposite direction as if detached from my body, but not hurting at all.

With my right hand I grabbed a fistful of my G-suit above the right thigh and pulled the leg forward to where it was supposed to be, next to the left one. My guess was that it was really disconnected from my body. It was only being kept "attached" by all the zippers of the G-suit. At about the same time, I realized that I couldn't move my left arm and that my left elbow was broken. My brain emblazoned the word TROUBLE in huge letters all across the sky.

I knew I needed time to think. I could slow down the streamlined velocity of my fall if I jettisoned the weight from my seat. So I made the decision to detach myself from it. Usually, this happens automatically when the pilot falls below 14,000 feet, but the disappointment of that upper ejection handle malfunction was still fresh in my mind. I had no desire to descend the rest of the way Mary Poppins-style straight into the arms of the hundreds of Egyptian who would surely be waiting for me. The pilot can free himself from the ejection seat by pulling on two metal rings at his waist, one below the other. So using my right hand alone, I unhooked the rings. First ring… second ring… all at once my shoulders received a forceful blow when my main parachute opened. And then, with my head bent slightly, I could see the empty seat making its way to the ground.

The good news, when you're suspended there at 15,000 feet, is that you don't feel any sensation of movement. You can even fool yourself into thinking that you'll just float up there forever. *Great, then what?* one might ask. But anyone who's ever traversed that final stretch to the gallows will tell you that any seeming delay is to be warmly welcomed.

Looking down, it appears that people are anticipating my arrival. There are three villages below, and from each one a serpent has started winding its way toward my projected landing spot. Looking up, it's easy to understand how they've spotted me. My parachute is made of bold red and white sections and, against the clear blue sky, is plainly visible from Marrakesh to Bangladesh.

So, not genuinely believing that I will remain up high forever, I rid myself of extraneous gear. As I do so, I start picturing scenes of the "Meanwhile, back in Israel…" type. My wife, my parents, my brothers, my pilot comrades—all flash before me without me being able to tell them how sorry

I am for ruining their day. I even think about the wonderful pair of moccasins I bought just a few days before at a store on Dizengoff Street. Looking at my dangling foot, I wonder if I'll be able to return them and get my money back, should I ever make it back to Tel Aviv.

I busy myself pulling out all the documents from the pockets of my G-suit, ripping them up and tossing them away. Kind of tricky with a broken left elbow, but it gives me something to do. Thus I part with the charts of call signs, lists of radio frequencies, maps, intercept control procedures and other such materials that would not exactly behoove a visitor like me to have in his possession in Egypt. By this time, it is clear that the villagers below are not indifferent to my arrival. Shouts arise from the three human snakes whose heads relentlessly advance toward our imagined meeting point as their tails seem to endlessly uncoil from within their respective hollows. To my surprise, my leg still doesn't hurt, and I start to think about how I might hit the ground without breaking the other leg.

Again I think about my family. Tomorrow is Rosh Hashanah Eve, and it is obvious that no matter what is about to happen, this Rosh Hashanah will be different for my family than any other in the past. Images of different people from Israel pass before my eyes.

Two

11-SEP-1969

M y attention shifts again to the condition of my leg. Gingerly, I insert my hand between the G-suit and the flight coverall. It feels like crushed meat. I withdraw my hand; wet blood covers my fingers. Now I start to feel the pain. Inside a pocket of the flight coverall, my hand had bumped against the commando knife that's usually attached to the right leg. I toss the knife away and try to think of any other items pilots carry with them that could give the impression of hostile intentions. The last thing I want is to further stoke the anger of the waiting crowd. Judging from the increasingly louder shouts from below, they are riled up enough as it is.

When you get down to about 2,000 feet, you can feel the ground approaching, and the rate of descent seems to accelerate with each passing second. The last part happens very fast. From about one hundred feet above, I can see that

I am going to hit near a group of black-clad women who are shrieking in horror and trying to scramble out of the way. And then I hit the ground.

I fall on my intact left leg while doing a half-somersault and then topple onto my back. I immediately free myself from the chute and begin to pick myself up. No part of my body will move. I am sprawled in a cotton field. The first thought that goes through my head, with the ingrained patriotism of someone raised during Israel's early days as a state, is that the cotton plants here are a lot lower and sparser than the ones at Kibbutz Yavne, which I used to pass on my way to Hatzor Airbase.

My emergency dinghy for water landings is lying all inflated to my left, and the lines that attach the pilot to it are tangled on my chest. My right hand instinctively reaches out to press on my broken left wrist to ease the pain. My right leg is lying atop my right shoulder, in the reverse of its natural position. The shoe is leaning on my right ear.

Within seconds, the first Egyptian villager is standing over me. *Min inta?* "Who are you?" he asks with much excitement. Talk about an open question. I ponder what answer will make him refrain from killing me—no easy task to gauge by the look on his face. The tumult escalates as more villagers press in towards me, shoving and yelling and trying to talk to me. Who am I, then, at this moment? A proud pilot who just twenty minutes earlier felt like the king of the sky, a feeling I'd enjoyed since the day I got my wings? Or a freshly plucked eagle at the mercy of an unfamiliar mob?

My notoriety in Israel may be why I feel mildly offended when that villager who asked me, "Who are you?" doesn't recognize me. But this is not the time to indulge my ego. It's the time to start implementing what we've discussed many times in the squadron, i.e.—if you are ever unlucky enough to fall into a land that devours uninvited visitors, stall for time. Don't communicate easily, certain that the enemy military or police will come to rescue you.

"Are you Egyptian?" the first villager asks in Arabic.

Someone else takes my leg that was resting on my shoulder and, in one swift movement, shifts it to its normal position. The pain shoots through my body and I cry out. The sound makes no impression on the crowd around me, which is quickly growing ever larger.

"Are you Russian?" is the next question.

"Water," I say in Arabic. I don't care if they kill me just as long as somebody gives me a little water first. Everything I've just been through has dried me out so much that all else is secondary to wetting my mouth.

Inta Sahyuni? "Are you a Zionist?" he persists in interrogating me, trying to be heard over the clamor around us and taking my silences up to this point to mean no. It surprises me that he uses the word Zionist and not Israeli. All I've read about the Arabs' denial of Israel's existence suddenly becomes reality. I wonder for a moment whether I ought to correct him on that, but pilots are generally clever fellows and don't tend to get into political arguments with people they don't know that well. So it's a good time to just say "water" once more and in an even more plaintive voice. Any uncontrolled response could expose my Zionist identity. And these are not the most favorable circumstances for that revelation.

The surrounding horde grows restless. The attempts to get near me grow more chaotic from one moment to the next. People step on me, fall on me, push in from all sides. My field of vision fills with the villagers' bare feet. I can feel them starting to undress me. First the shoes and then the socks. When they reach my G-suit with all its complicated zippers, I lift my head to help them see how to get it off, and in doing so glimpse the bloody red color of my right thigh. My head drops back into a helpless position. I hear myself asking for water again.

The *Min inta?* guy keeps at it insistently. He tries one country after another—France, England, America, even Syria. And the more he asks, the more I repeat my request for water. My thirst overwhelms me. My left arm screams, and I can feel that someone with a more practical bent has skipped the shoes and socks and gone straight for the real treasure, my watch. I clench my fingers to make the job easier for him, if only so he won't need to use any more rough movements to collect the spoils.

The mob now completely encircles me. Those in the outer rings begin shouting, "Kill him, kill him!" while those in the innermost circle shout back, "He's an Egyptian!" But the attempts to confirm my origins continue.

Ten minutes after I've landed, while rummaging through my clothes, somebody notices the tag sewn onto my undershirt. And the Hebrew writing on it.

"He's a Jew! He's a Jew!"

Three

11-SEP-1969

The people nearest me—all of them barefoot, with darkly tanned legs protruding from white *galabiyas*— fall silent. As the uproar from the ones further out grows even louder, those in the inner circle move away from me. The space around me widens for a moment, and I am able to see their faces as they behold their very first Israeli. Only then do I notice that each of them is armed with some kind of farming implement: pitchfork, hoe, scythe. No one has shown up for this meeting empty-handed. And here I am at their feet, with a broken leg and broken arm, stuck on my back, a defenseless Israeli among hundreds of Egyptian villagers. The jolt of surprise soon fades, and then the dispute over my fate resumes with greater urgency.

It's clear that the mob has divided into two camps. Those who want to kill me keep shouting my true identity, and those who want to protect me shout that I am an Egyptian pilot. The struggle between the two groups intensifies. From somewhere, a boy of about fourteen manages to squeeze his way through all of the adults and reaches me. Keeping up a stream of Arabic curses, before anyone can do anything, he strikes me in the face with a large rock. I manage to turn my head a fraction of a second before the rock hits me square in the face. My left eyebrow takes the brunt of the blow and slices open. Blood flows into my eye, slides down my nose and paints my cheeks.

This is how a lynching begins, I think.

The sensation is akin to a burn. My right hand reflexively shoots up to wipe my eye. As soon as it lets go of my broken left wrist, though, a sharper current of pain is dispatched from my broken elbow. I have to abandon the attempt to stanch the blood flow and return my right hand to its indispensable job as a pain-reliever. At the same time, the pain from my shattered thigh is intensifying to ever more agonizing levels. In short, my physical condition has never been worse.

Strangely enough, the episode with the boy humanizes me. Not only is the stoner thrown out by the adults, but a towel appears from somewhere and a young man of about twenty-five kneels beside me. He cleans the blood from my face and un-blinds my blood-drenched eye. He then takes the bloodstained towel and ties it around my right thigh, just above the ever widening femoral pool. It isn't top-flight medical treatment, not even quite a tourniquet, but the message is clear. If the worst is going to happen, it will not happen here. Not now.

After an hour's worth of debate, the tenor of the cotton field changes and a new purposefulness takes hold. Four men hoist me onto their shoulders. The crowd moves aside to create a path. Trailed by a throng of about a thousand people, my bearers take me to the nearest village. I can't see the mass since I am being carried face forward, but I can clearly hear their deafening chant. "Nasser! Nasser!" they begin shouting, louder and louder, as if informing the president of the republic of the delivery of a sacrificial lamb.

My thoughts focus again on the pain coming from my mangled leg. It's getting worse by the moment, especially whenever one of the men carrying me stumbles in the rutted field and the leg is jerked around—bending not at the knee but at some odd point further up the thigh. I'm surprised that I'm not passing out, and it even occurs to me that I am alert enough to handle a game of chess. I review my situation up to this point, and as strange as it may be, I feel my confidence returning. I arrived here an hour ago, immobile. I survived the wild encounter with the locals. The odds that I will be passed from the villagers into the care of the authorities appear to be improving. Despite my injuries, I am in complete control of my faculties. I've been able to follow what is happening around me. I haven't lost my cool. I haven't shown any signs of weakness beyond my physical limitations, and at no point have I asked for mercy. My most immediate agitation is desperate thirst, and so the only word I've used is "water" in Arabic.

We come to one of the villages I spotted during my descent. The procession now makes its way down a narrow passageway between two rows of mud-and-mortar houses. A trickle of sewage flows alongside the houses, and chickens scurry about before us making a racket with their screeching. My bearers turn left and enter the yard of one of the houses. A donkey lying on a pile of straw is sent off with a kick, and I am set down in its place. A dozen men come into the yard with me. I take them to be the village elders. The rest of the throng remains outside the compound. Some crowd onto the adjacent rooftops.

The dozen try to speak to me. I gaze at them and ask for water. My thoughts wander to my wife, Miriam. I wonder whether she already knows that I won't be coming home tonight, and if she doesn't, how long will she continue to live under the illusion that all is well with our family.

The yard tends to offer a feeling of calm, and that feeling is enhanced by the relative quiet that envelops us and by the non-menacing faces of the small group here. The only thing they want is for me to speak. And the only thing I want is to let time pass in the hope that the Egyptian security forces are aware by now that I am in the village and are on their way. "Water," is my sole request, and they in fact bring out a jug of water and place it near my head.

"You tell us water, we give you water," the young man who wrapped the towel around my leg in the field keeps repeating in broken English. But I stubbornly reserve the right to remain silent and do not engage him in conversation. I don't actually get to drink any water from the jug and just lie there silently in the yard staring up at the people sitting on the rooftops while ignoring those on the ground. The relative calm allows my mind to turn over. It's now starting to digest the fact that I've fallen into captivity at the height of the War of Attrition, Eqypt and Israel's bloody dance after their Six Day War in 1967.

I've withstood some tough tests before. This isn't the first time I've been hit by enemy fire. But just making it to this ass' bed has been by far the worst. Now that I am about to be "saved" by the Egyptian military, the reality that I am in for far greater torments begins to weigh on me. The odds of withstanding them with dignity are much more daunting.

As I lay here in silence, one of the elders does a more thorough search of the numerous pockets in my flight coverall. He goes through pocket after pocket until he opens my left sleeve and finds my pay stub for the month of August. A whoop of joy is heard in the yard, and I understand that when the time for questioning comes, the information on that stub will be critical to my survival. Exactly what is written on it, I do not remember. I just know that I must prepare myself for whatever it is.

I say nothing and after the hubbub dies down, neither do the others. Someone comes into the yard and says something in Arabic. Once more the men pick me up on their shoulders. The convoy sets out again. Unlike the first trip, this time I am carried with my head facing backward, so I have a view of my multitude of escorts. I can't shake a slight suspicion that I am being taken to a makeshift gallows that was prepared while I was in the yard, perhaps on one of those broad-trunked trees I spied on our way into the village before. And then it strikes me that this parade could be a dress rehearsal for my upcoming funeral procession. This time the young people of the village walk in front. All along the way they play with my toes, twisting them until I give a yelp of pain, which triggers a bout of childish laughter. And then the game repeats with twisting my toes the other way until I give up another cry of pain, and more laughter, and so on. We move along for about ten minutes and then the march comes to a stop. To my right I spot a military pickup. Beside it stand six soldiers in dark blue berets.

The throng does not release me easily to the blue berets. I am put into the truck, but the vehicle is rocked by the surrounding crowd, and it takes quite some time to get free of them. Night has almost fallen as I lie on the floor of the moving truck. The six soldiers sit on either side of me, rifles between their legs, silently fixing me with curious stares. Their dark blue berets look enormous, and for a moment I find it amusing. But now that the threat of immediate execution is behind me, the cold hard awareness sets in—Egypt, captivity, serious injury, medical treatment, unlimited time, interrogations, guards, War of Attrition, isolation.

It'll be okay, I tell myself.

The truck slows and we enter a walled yard surrounding a one-story building. Men are standing there, waiting in silence, some in khaki uniforms, others in white robes. A stretcher appears and conveys me from the truck and into a long lighted corridor. An officer comes up to me and asks me to identify myself. "Giora Romm, Captain, Serial Number 484515, Blood Type B," I hear myself say. A shiver goes through me. *You're speaking with your captors. Control yourself, control yourself.* But there is nothing more. An IV is attached to my right arm.

After a while, the officer comes back and informs me that I am in a hospital in a small city, and everyone is waiting for the surgeon to arrive. The gurney is pushed along again and this time it stops in the center of a large, brightly-lit room. I look down the length of my body and give myself the once-over. I'm not at my best. My flight coverall is torn and caked with dirt. A dark, dried bloodstain covers the fabric over the right thigh. Two filthy feet stick out at the bottom, the right one streaked all over with blood. I can reach up with my hand and feel my sand-filled hair and the clotted blood on my face.

I'm not sure how long I lie like that in the room. Officers come and go. Pilots in flight suits also come in, stand beside me briefly and then leave. Nobody who comes in tries to talk to me. They just come in, look at me, and leave. And then, finally, the surgeon appears, or as they called him—"the bone specialist." Within minutes, he has me hooked up to the anesthesia apparatus. It's a lovely way to end the day.

Four

12-SEP-1969

When I open my eyes, I am lying in bed in a dark room. Oddly enough, I know right away that I am a POW in Egypt. A male nurse in white uniform sits on a chair next to the bed. When he sees me moving, he gets up and asks how I am feeling. I tell him I am thirsty and ask for water. His second question is, "Who burned the Al Aqsa mosque?"

A few months before, a mentally disturbed tourist from Australia visiting Jerusalem tried to torch the Al Aqsa mosque on the Temple Mount—a sacred site for the entire Muslim world. Had he succeeded, not only the mosque but the entire region would have been set alight.

"Not me," I answer him dryly, in a tone that says, "leave me alone." I can hardly believe my ears but appreciate the quick lesson on the religious sensitivities of my captors. Despite his position in the healing trade, I can see that he will not be a supportive person to talk to. My eyes begin to adjust to the darkness, and I assess my post-operative situation.

My right leg is in an iron brace, my left arm is completely encased in an ordinary plaster cast and my left eyebrow, where the rock made a large cut, is stitched up and bandaged. The nurse finally responds to my request. He takes a tongue depressor wrapped in gauze, dips it in a glass of water and lets me suck on it as much as I can.

A group of people enter the room. Someone opens the blinds a little, and I catch a glimpse of a wristwatch that reads five o'clock. Again the gurney is brought to the room, but this time there is also a blindfold for my eyes.

Before long, I am on the floor of a minibus together with the same bunch that entered my room at dawn. They chat with one another and let me suck on the tongue depressor from time to time. After about a two-hour drive, we enter another compound. This I can tell from the squeaking of the iron hinges of the entrance gate. I am taken along on the gurney, and by the dwindling amount of light that penetrates the blindfold, I gather that we've gone inside a building.

I hear the sound of a door opening. The complicated and somewhat precarious maneuvers that ensue, replete with much lifting and tilting of the stretcher, indicate to me that we are turning out of a very narrow hallway into our final destination. When the stretcher returns to its horizontal position I am carefully removed from it and then my back meets a cold concrete floor. Without saying a word, the men leave what I take to be a room and shut the door. The sound of one key after another being turned makes it plain that from here—I will not be escaping.

I tear the blindfold from my eyes with my one good hand. Nothing changes. I am enveloped in pitch blackness, and the darkness and total silence give me the feeling that I will be left alone indefinitely. There is no telling when anyone will come to see me again, if ever.

My eyes gradually adjust to the gloom. When I look to my left, I can make out the vague outlines of a bathtub about three feet away. My thirst is now the only thing dictating my actions. I know I must get to that tub no matter what. How will I reach the faucets once I got there? I'll solve that problem when I come to it. Is it even possible to get there? How can I even move across the rough concrete floor with my right leg in this iron contraption and my left arm broken? It is doable, but long and slow. For more than half an hour, I struggle to move myself toward the bathtub. With each tiny bit of progress, all that gives me strength to go on is the thought of the moment when I will reach the tap. At long last, I cover the final inches and reach out with my right hand to touch the object of my desperate desire. What I feel is concrete. I roll over on my left side and reach up to the top part of the tub. More concrete.

Evidently, they don't install you in a bathroom on the first stop of your journey as a captive. The "bathtub" is just an elevated section of the concrete floor, a makeshift bed in the cell where I am imprisoned. I roll back onto my back, knowing there is nothing I can do now but lie here and wait.

Fighting the thirst, I try to put my thoughts in order. First I think about what is happening right now in Israel in connection with my disappearance. Because of the violent nature of the blow to my aircraft and the need to eject immediately, I didn't have time to report it over the radio. So I presume that no one in Israel knows of my fate.

When the door to the small cell finally opens, my heart pounds.

The second stage is about to begin, the meeting with the professionals. Into the cell come the prison doctor and his personal servant. The doctor is dressed like a model officer in a perfectly pressed uniform studded with more medals than one would expect for someone serving in an army that hasn't won a war in quite some time. His spiffy attire underscores the distance between us—there he stands with his exemplary appearance and here I lie, flat at his feet, still in my ratty flight coverall and undershirt smeared with mud and blood. He asks me a question or two about my physical condition and then launches into a little speech about what wonders cooperation on the part of the prisoner can do for his chances of recovery.

I tell him that I'm thirsty. He sends his servant to bring me a cup of tea "with lots of sugar." I ask him when I will go to the hospital, but he just resumes his lecture about cooperation. You don't have to be a military expert to know that what captivity really comes down to is a struggle over the information in the prisoner's possession. But you don't necessarily expect the medical staff to be a part of this battle. I take an immediate dislike to this fellow; though I realize it is still too early to develop personal taste to people I meet.

The servant returns with the cup of tea. I can't wait even a second and gulp the whole thing down in one shot. With my head still tilted backward, I immediately throw up the entire contents of my stomach, soiling myself more, and worse, staining the doctor's shiny shoes. He spins around and exits the cell as his aghast servant hurriedly trails behind, leaving me there on the floor, my thirst momentarily slaked.

The light bulb over my head, which was switched on when the doctor entered the cell, remains lit, so I am no longer in darkness. I inventory the cell. It is about six feet wide and eight feet long. To my left is that concrete "bathtub" which is meant to serve as a bed. The floor and bed are the usual gray concrete color. The cell door is painted light blue and has a small window in the upper section for observing the prisoner, and the ceiling high above me is made of asbestos. It doesn't take a musical ear to identify the sound of rats skittering back and forth atop the asbestos panels.

Now it is time to start dispelling the other darkness that surrounds me, the uncertainty of my future. Everyone who takes risks says to himself, *It won't happen to me.* But it has happened. I know I have to begin constructing the picture of my new world. I study the cell, commit it to memory. I notice Arabic words scratched into the whitewashed walls on either side of me and wonder what became of the cell's previous occupants. I see that many layers of paint cover the door in front of me, and when I turn my head to look behind I see that in the upper part of the wall is a small window covered with wooden boards. The only thing that seems alive in this cell is the bulb that dangles above me at the end of a twisted electrical cord. Sometimes I have the feeling that as I stare at the bulb it stares back at me, and maybe laughs too.

Five

12-SEP-1969

My cell door opens and a man in his twenties, in civilian dress, enters and sits down on the bed, smiling amiably.

"I am Sayeed and I am in charge of you. I was sent to make sure that you receive proper medical care because of your serious injuries."

He speaks English well, with a pronounced Arabic accent. He is of medium height, his face is pockmarked with what appear to be acne scars, and he wears a gold watch. He does not stop smiling, which makes the atmosphere in the cell much more pleasant.

"I am a pilot, I am an officer, I am a captain in the Israeli Air Force, and I want medical treatment," I say.

"No problem," he replies. "There's just one formality we need to get out of the way and it's being taken care of right now." He, too, starts talking about cooperation and about how

I have nothing to fear because of Egypt's glorious tradition of taking excellent care of its POWs. It seems like he is trying to convince me that I should actually be glad to be here with him rather than in Tel Aviv. My sense is that we are in the warm-up stage before the start of the real game.

Now Sayeed turns more serious and businesslike and says that we have to hurry up and get me to the hospital in Cairo if I want to save my leg.

"I am a pilot, I am an officer, I am a captain in the Israeli Air Force, and I want medical treatment." I know I must come up with a kind of mantra that I can repeat over and over again that can serve me as an anchor in the hours to come.

"No problem. We'll just fill out the hospital admission form and we'll be on our way to Cairo." He pulls a pencil and some sort of card out of his pocket and asks me the four first questions of a POW: name, rank, serial number and blood type. In the same exact tone, he proceeds to the fifth question: squadron number.

My heart rate doubles. *Here it is, the moment of truth. They want something I'm not supposed to give them.* Here in this small cell, in the space of less than ten minutes, I've already been subjected to the "good cop/bad cop" routine, and from just one man.

"The hospital doesn't need that sort of information in order to treat an injured patient."

"Maybe not in Israel, but in Egypt it's part of the process, and we're not going to change it just for you."

I give him the "I am a pilot, I am an officer" mantra once again. He says that the prison's only ambulance is waiting outside. If it leaves empty it won't be back until the next morning.

I won't answer his question for two reasons. First, I've been trained not to give away information. Second, I'm insulted by the casual way they are dealing with me. The "business as usual" manner in which he posed the question and the simple way in which he tried to extract classified information is disrespectful. This cheap fiction about the hospital form (as if I, an ace Israeli fighter pilot, were that gullible) and his ever-present smile strongly influence the most important decisions I must make as a prisoner—what sort of image I am going to present, what position I am going to take, and whether I am prepared for a long and arduous journey strewn with terrible risks and agonies.

As I am busy sorting my thoughts, Sayeed stands up and fixes me with a serious, rather menacing look. He tells me I have just made my first mistake and leaves the room.

Six

11-Apr-1961

I was a student in the eleventh grade of a military boarding school, the Reali School in Haifa, a secondary school version of West Point. It was the year of the Adolph Eichmann trial. Because there was no television in Israel yet, we all sat and listened to the opening session of the proceedings on the radio. Then we went back to school, and during the afternoons, from time to time, we heard more testimony. We were young men, seventeen years old, who had never spoken about the Holocaust. We practically ignored it.

About twenty-five of us were sitting and listening, and we heard the voice of a woman who told about standing behind a truck on which her two sons were being taken away. She was screaming, and a German guard stopped the truck, turned to her and told her, "Well, lady, you can pick one of them."

Unlike Sophie in William Styron's novel *Sophie's Choice* who chose her son over her daughter, this woman didn't pick either one. The truck left with both boys on board. When the testimony was over and the room was silent, one of us, who was known for being even quieter than the rest of us, stood up and said suddenly, "I cannot take it any more," and he left the room.

My father came to Israel in 1925 when just a teenager, as did my mother five years later. Hitler was still a non-personality trying to write his Mein Kampf and maybe painting his masterpiece in Austria. At that time, there was no aggressive threat to Jews as much as there was a concept of trying to build a new kind of Judaism in Palestine. There was no feeling of any pressure or urgency either.

When the Nazis first came to power, it was not annihilation they had in mind but more of an ethnic cleansing. They wanted to purge Europe of Jews, whom they perceived as a destructive element. For a very short while there was the Madagascar Plan—namely, to move all the nine million Jews of Europe to the island of Madagascar—a plan which very rapidly proved to be unrealistic. Then the Jews began to be encouraged, if you want to call it encouraged, to leave Germany. Of course, they had to leave everything behind, all of their friends, property, and history.

As time went by, it became clear that ethnic cleansing was not a viable solution if Europe was to be totally cleansed of Jews. The move to genocide was almost inevitable. In January 1942, during the Wannsee Conference, the decision was very clearly made. The Germans would systematically clean Europe of Jews through extermination.

It then became, if you will, a huge logistical problem.

First, they had to decide how to run the deception operation. It didn't prove all that difficult. Jews, like many other people, refused to believe that with each sunrise they were very near their final day. There were transportation problems too. They also had to find a solution that enabled extermination en masse, so Zyklon B gas took its infamous place in history. And there was the problem of disposing of corpses—so they put very efficient German people on the job who created the crematorium mechanism. This began a process through which six million people, 1.5 million of them children, lost their lives.

In the outer circle, there was not a lot of help. The allies who began to learn more and more about what was going on in Europe decided not to allocate any military resources to stopping or slowing down the genocide. There was no bombing of the camps, no attacking of the trains, no sabotaging of the railways.

Even when something known as "trucks for blood" was considered—namely, a deal to try to save the Jews of Hungary for 10,000 trucks—there was a complete refusal on the side of the British to supply these trucks, which would have saved over 100,000 Hungarian Jews.

I tried to think what a Jew would have felt during these horrible years. Anxiety seems to me as too weak a word. Maybe fear. Maybe desperation. There were some heroic attempts at resistance, the most famous of which was the Warsaw Ghetto Uprising. But by and large, there was a wide sense of helplessness. There was literally nobody to turn to.

When Germany fell, 1.5 million Jews found themselves behind the Iron Curtain. Understanding that Europe was no longer a safe place, these Jews began to look for ways to get to Palestine. It seemed reasonable to assume that after World War II, when the magnitude of the catastrophe would be revealed to all, getting to Palestine would be no problem. But, in the three years between '45 and '48, strange phenomena occurred. The British, who ruled Palestine during that time, refused entry to the Jews. Ships were intercepted in the high seas and turned back to Europe or to new camps—called displaced person camps—in Cyprus. I believe the most famous of these ships, but not the only one, was the Exodus, where 4,500 Jews packed onto an old ship tried to make their way to Israel.

As the story goes, they were stopped by the British and tried to resist. The British then stormed the ship, killed some of the Jews, and turned the ship back to Europe.

As a reaction to the fear, the desperation, the anxiety, the loneliness, and the helplessness of these years, there developed in Palestine, now Israel, a very deep resolve.

The people said, "We must have our own country; we must take care of ourselves; we cannot expect anybody else to assist us." So we declared our independence in May 1948. Immediately afterwards, we found ourselves in an eighteen month war with seven armies, with an embargo from the United States. We did get some help from the Soviet Union—the irony of history. We lost one percent of our population. This is as if the US would have lost 1.5 million Americans during World War II, five times as many as the actual losses were. Then one day the war was over, and there was a new Israel.

During the '50s I was a child. I didn't know anything about the Holocaust. I thought I was raised in a normal country. I learned later that I was living through a melting pot period—a very intensive number of immigration years in which we multiplied our population, expanding our demographic base with Jews from Iraq, North Africa, and elsewhere. We wanted to create a situation by which Israel would be able to build itself. And, we really felt that we were building the "new" Israel.

Before the Eichmann trial, my classmates and I didn't know who all these strange people were with their six digit numbers tattooed on their arms. Now we did.

The three years I spent at the military boarding school, from tenth through twelfth grade, were critical in shaping my personality as a fighter. We were a class of twenty-seven, and we were, so they say, the finest class to ever graduate.

It was a select group, one could see even then, although we were still teenagers. Not only people like Lieutenant General Amnon Lipkin-Shahak, Major General Matan Vilnai, and

Brigadier General Yomtov Tamir, but also many who fell in Israel's wars, those wars that came upon us so frequently in our first years in the Israeli Defense Force (IDF). These were extremely impressive people, each in his own way. Young men who likely would have gone far in Israeli society had they not been killed.

Our three years together was not an easy time. Beyond the high demands made upon the individual, which was a basic part of Israeli culture in those days, we imposed upon ourselves, and the school also imposed upon us, especially high standards of achievement. In the mornings we attended the high school, an institution that didn't cut anyone any slack, and in the afternoons we led a rigid and highly regimented military lifestyle. A large portion of our school vacations were devoted to actual military training, and all of this took place in an atmosphere of strict discipline and Spartan ideology.

By the end of twelfth grade, if there was one thing we internalized and took with us from those three years, it was the recognition that the mission—no matter in what area—must be accomplished. Nothing aside from the report "Mission accomplished" would ever be acceptable. It's hard for me to compare the strenuous training we underwent there to anything that exists today. Always in conditions of making do with little, always with the attitude of "at any cost and using what's available" and always with mutual support and friendship that grew stronger from day to day, even while interlaced with a constant sense of competition among us, at times overt and at times hidden, to be the very best of all.

Ehud Shani, the most accomplished student in our class, was killed as an outstanding company commander in the paratroops in the Six Day War. Lieutenant Danny Engel, the quiet one who could not take listening to the trial testimony of the woman who lost her two sons, crashed with his Super Mystere plane in the first attack on the Inshas Air Base near

Cairo in the same war. Adam Weiler, who interrupted his studies at Sussex University in England and returned to be a company commander in the armored corps, and Nadav Klein, who was already a reservist in the Golani Brigade and was the guy we all had tapped to become a government minister at the very least, were killed in the War of Attrition, the first at the Canal and the second in the Jordan Rift Valley.

Dubi Dror, a Golani battalion commander, was killed in the attempt to take Mount Hermon in the Yom Kippur War. None of us would compromise when it came to being at the forefront of the effort, and none of us would compromise in striving to accomplish the mission—always in the spirit of our boarding school credo: "With Calm and Confidence."

There's something extraordinary about the decision to leave home at high school age and join a boarding school, all the more so one with a military character. I don't recall us boys ever having any discussions about what compelled each one of us to make this move. To us it apparently seemed quite the simple and obvious choice. At the time, military service seemed crucial to the country's survival, and the military was an organization that had true prestige, with absolutely nothing artificial or showy about it.

Above all, the military imparted a sense of destiny and self-pride, something that is sorely lacking today, and we wanted to be a part of this organization and to go far in it. As clear as it was to us, it was not at all simple to explain to other people. Our families supported us the way that families support their dear sons. But our friends, both back home, wherever that happened to be, and at the Reali High School in Haifa, demanded further explanations and prodded us with typical teenage crudeness and sarcasm. But we kept to ourselves, almost like a sect elevated above the rest, a sect with a unique calling, a sect that had to prepare each one of its members for service at the highest conceivable levels.

Seven

12-SEP-1969

I lie here in the lighted cell, aware that—to borrow air combat terminology—I have now reached the stage of the dogfight where I am in very tight maneuvers with my Egyptian captors. Can I hold just the right fighting position to maintain an edge over them? What will help me keep my nose up without stalling and going into a spin? Will the "I am a pilot, I am an officer" mantra give me the needed energy? Do I have any other ammunition at my disposal? Is it even possible to plan in this situation, or will I just have to have faith that alertness and quick thinking will get me through whatever lies ahead?

As I am trying to come up with a strategy, the cell door opens and four soldiers are standing there with my usual vehicle, the stretcher. My eyes are covered once more, this time not with a hospital dressing but with a blindfold made expressly for this purpose, a sign that I am in a facility that has seen a prisoner or two before. Being loaded onto the stretcher and maneuvered out the door into the narrow hallway is a bit harrowing, especially blindfolded, for if anyone here is going to end up on the floor, it's me. But that's not the heart of the matter. The real question is where are they taking me? Will I find myself in an ambulance on the way to the hospital, and so learn that Sayeed is not such a serious adversary after all? Or will the pressure now be ratcheted up, and *my* seriousness as an adversary put to the test?

The soldiers transporting the stretcher cover a good patch of ground, and my inner clock tells me that we've already been on the move for longer than it took this morning to get from the ambulance to the cell. Now we're entering a room, and I'm carefully lifted off the stretcher by the soldiers and lowered. Before I can begin speculating on the possibilities, my back touches down on an incredibly soft mattress and, still blindfolded, I immediately register that I am on a wide and comfortable bed. The blindfold is removed and I see that I am in a large room with light green curtains. In the center of the room is a table, between the table and the bed are some chairs, and beside them stand four middle-aged men in civilian dress, all gazing at me intently.

One of them starts talking to me, inquiring as to how I feel and quickly steering the conversation to the connection between medical care for my leg, which all in the room agree is in very bad shape, and my behavior as a prisoner— or put more bluntly, my willingness to provide information. We speak English, which I have chosen as the language of communication between us. Sticking to Hebrew might have been the more advisable move in captivity, but I am sure (or at least so I hope) that eventually I will get to the hospital and there I will have to be able to communicate with whoever might try to save my leg and my arm.

A pitcher is placed on a stool beside the bed, and I ask to drink. It's lemonade made from tiny sweet lemons, and I have never found anything anywhere else whose taste compares. I drink glass after glass. I'm still thirsty but I stop myself so as not to look like someone who can't get a grip on his distress.

So it's my leg that's going to be their weapon in the first round, I tell myself, as I also wonder how I'll know how much rope I have to work with here and just how far I can stretch it. The contrast between this room and the cell just goes to show what a wide range of options my captors have to choose from, and I sense that I have yet to be exposed to their entire arsenal. They want to know why I'm unwilling to fill out the hospital admission form. I repeat the claim that in Israel there is no such form and try to see when I can give them the "I am a pilot, I am an officer" chorus once more.

From my "if you get shot down and are a Prisoner of War instruction" I know that a captive continually moves—or to put it better—is moved, from one new world to another, and must formulate his relationship to it each time afresh. A constant application of uncertainty and disorientation is a key instrument in the interrogator's toolbox. A panicked prisoner is virtually incapable of withholding information. While I'm still trying to orient myself in this new world, two soldiers enter the room. One comes up to me, pulls down the blanket, cleans the last bits of dirt and vomit from my filthy chest and carefully helps me into a white undershirt. The other is holding a camera and he takes about ten pictures of me.

The fact that as of this moment there is documentation of my presence in Egypt is immediately entered into the "pros" column of the situation, meager as it might be compared to the "cons." I don't know where these pictures are headed, and I certainly don't ask, but the brief pause gives me a chance to take a closer look at the four men in the room. All four are in civilian attire, all have swarthy complexions and mustaches, and all seem a bit excited. A feeling of confidence comes over me—confidence that death is not on the docket just now. It's a huge relief, though I can't revel in it too much. The case is still rich with possibilities, none of which are very consoling.

The two soldiers leave and one of the men resumes talking with me. The conversation revolves around my foolish refusal to fill out the hospital admission form. Sayeed, the intelligence officer, who has been sitting in a corner up to now, gets up and walks to the center of the room. He is holding a bundle of papers and clearly wants to get back in the picture. They ask me if I know Nissim Ashkenazi. His plane was downed three weeks earlier.

This is an easy question. Of course I don't know him. I have nothing to do with him. I don't need to convince myself that I don't know him. I only need to remind myself that I have just stepped into the great "Hall of Lies and Falsehoods" in which I must pace back and forth without the thundering of my heart being heard all over Cairo.

Nissim is a bit older than me. He and I flew together for a year in the Super Mystere squadron at Hatzor. He was the commander of the first Skyhawk squadron at Hatzerim and, as it turns out, the day before his plane was downed, I had cleared out of my apartment in the family housing section there so that he could move in. But here, in Egyptian captivity, I do not know him, and I say so loudly and clearly. Riding this little wave of confidence, I proceed to ask how he is. This is just the sort of rookie mistake they were waiting for.

"He was badly injured, but because he is cooperating fully he is receiving topnotch medical care. He'll be fine."

Taking immediate mental note of this error, I resolve to show more restraint from now on when I get the impulse to make small talk. I picture Nissim's face. He's Bulgarian. He's a redhead. He has a mustache. If he's "cooperating" with them, it must be some other fellow who landed in Egypt. Nissim barely cooperates with his friends (the few that pass his admission standards). Still, I'm worried. I know that he has fallen into captivity. How will he know that I am here? How will he know not to get me into trouble with his answers in the interrogations to which he is surely being subjected?

The door opens and a short man in civilian dress enters, with a fearsomely stern expression on his face. He looks me over, avoiding eye contact, says something to the others in Arabic and sits down on a chair near my bed, behind my head. The atmosphere in the room turns more serious.

The conversation resumes and Sayeed tells me that all they need is civilian information. I say I am willing to hear about the sections that need to be filled in on the form that they show me. The form resembles a questionnaire for applying to a sensitive position in the IDF. There are questions about family members, addresses, phone numbers and so on.

I distort fact after fact, except for certain things that I'm sure will come to light later on, such as my wife's name (when she writes me letters) or my parents' names. My mind is working feverishly. On the one hand, I don't know what a real interrogation looks like, and on the other hand, I'm amassing lies at an ever-increasing rate, and I presume I'll be compelled to repeat them many times, if only to test my credibility. Just talking about my family in Israel makes me feel like I'm selling them down the river, and I search for a way to alleviate this feeling. I distort addresses and telephone numbers and whatever they throw at me. While doing so, I invent "rules of lying" that are meant to help me if this kind of questioning is ever repeated. I try to do this visually and methodically.

I switch my parents' address with another address that's familiar to me. I change the last digit of each phone number.

I try to slow down the pace—I sip glass after glass of the delicious lemonade, I complain about pain from my injuries, I even ask for a break.

The whole time the boss, who I learn later was the head of Egyptian intelligence, General Sadeq, who went on to become Chief of General Staff, is sitting behind the head of the bed. I can't see him, but I'm not trying to win any new friends at the moment. He doesn't say a word and leaves all the work to the four interrogators and Sayeed.

And then, casually tossed into the flow of the civilian questions, comes a question relating to military matters. I stop and say that I cannot provide military information. That I believed them when they said it was an ordinary pre-hospitalization form, and that they are not being true to their word. The atmosphere in the room changes in an instant. One of the four, who has a threatening demeanor, gets up and starts speaking Arabic quickly and harshly. A discussion ensues.

Serious. Frightening.

One of the quartet, a scrawny fellow in a funny-looking jacket, comes over to me to resume the dialogue which had been going so nicely up to now, as he puts it. Speaking softly, he tells me that I will not be transferred to the hospital until I fill out the entire questionnaire. I repeat what I said before. I cannot answer questions about military matters. Sadeq gets up, strides to the middle of the room and stares at me. I look into his eyes. I have no idea who he is or what's going through his mind. But it's abundantly clear that he is the most senior person in the room. He barks out a few words in Arabic, turns and leaves.

The four interrogators follow him out of the room. I am left alone with Sayeed, and he tells me that from now on, I bear the responsibility for my medical condition. I repeat the key sentence, "I am a pilot, I am an officer, I am a captain in the Israeli Air Force, and I want medical treatment," and fall silent.

The door opens and four soldiers enter with the gurney. They blindfold me again, load me onto it and off we go. The way from the room to the cellblock passes through the prison yard. It's afternoon now and the sun penetrates the blindfold and momentarily gives me the feeling that I am free. I am outside. But soon we are back in the narrow hallway and once again there is the complicated maneuver to get me into the cell, and once again I am on the floor, and once again the soldiers leave. The door is locked.

With my right hand, I tear off the blindfold to find that I am back in the same cell. The concrete floor, the concrete bed, the lone bulb burning six feet above me, the asbestos ceiling, my leg inside the iron splint, my broken elbow and my stitched-up brow. I'm overwhelmed by a feeling of unfairness, but obviously there's not much I can do about it.

An hour passes, so I estimate, and nothing happens. Another hour passes and still I am all alone. I hear sounds from outside. The sounds of normal life. Footsteps in the yard, the noise of a passing train, prayers over the prison loudspeaker. With a loud jangle of keys, someone unlocks another one of the cells, a prisoner is dragged out, and he moans in Arabic. There is much silence between one sound and another. The terrible thirst hits me again and I sink into thoughts about what is happening back in Israel.

I work on memorizing all the personal information I gave them, and suddenly a simple pencil and paper seem like a fantastic dream. I am wearing an Egyptian undershirt. To me it symbolizes the new land to which I have come. How long will I be in captivity? My cell is the westernmost one in the cellblock, and the afternoon sun warms the wall. Heat seeps into the cell and the changing temperature gives the feeling that time is passing.

Later, the little panel in the door slides open, and an eye peeks into the cell. The panel closes, the door opens and Sayeed is standing there.

"It's the end of the workday, and the ambulance is about to leave for Cairo. If you're not in it today, you'll be here in the cell until tomorrow at least. You're making a mistake by being so stubborn, and you're causing yourself harm."

"I am a pilot, I am an officer, I am a captain in the Israeli Air Force, and I want medical treatment." Weakness is spreading through my body. I can tell I have a rising fever. Deep down I'm terrified by my overall situation, not just my medical condition. The smells, the sounds, the music over the prison loudspeakers, the call of the muezzin—all leave no doubt that I am in an Arab country.

But the recognition is still sinking in: Me, a captive? Me? One of the elite few chosen for the first course in flying Phantom jets when those planes first arrived in Israel? How could this be happening to me? Where did I go wrong?

Eight

12-SEP-1969

The door opens. Sayeed and two of my four interrogators from earlier are standing in the doorway. They offer me a deal—I will receive medical care. When I recover, I will cooperate and answer all of their questions. When they are satisfied, a Red Cross representative will come to see me.

I realize right away that what I have just been offered exceeds all my wildest dreams. I'm in quite a state of shock. But I act like I'm weighing the offer and after a decent pause I accept it. They are wary. "How do we know that you will honor the agreement?"

"An Israel pilot never lies," I reply indignantly.

They give Sayeed a brief order and head back out to the hallway. A minute later, one of them returns to the cell and addresses me in Hebrew, "And if there are things that you know that we don't ask about, it's important that you tell us those too. You will do that?"

"Certainly," I answer him. "If I am satisfied with the medical care, I will fulfill my commitments as an officer." *Hebrew? He speaks Hebrew?*

By the time I am taken outside to the ambulance, which is actually just an old minibus, it is evening. Through the slits in the blindfold I can see that it is dark now. I am laid on the floor of the minibus, on a blanket this time, and we set off on a bumpy ride, to the hospital apparently. To get there we drive through the streets of Cairo. All the noises of the city penetrate the minibus and I know that nobody around is aware that here inside this rickety vehicle lies the Israeli pilot whom they may have already heard about on the news.

They take me out of the vehicle and place me, still blindfolded, on a hospital gurney. When the gurney starts to move I stick out my right hand, the only limb I can move, and tear the blindfold off my face. We are just coming through the hospital's main entrance. We are in a large entry hall with round green pillars about three feet in diameter running straight from floor to ceiling. I am being transported on the gurney by two male nurses in white uniforms. The people in the entry hall look at me, but just as a way to pass the time while waiting in line, not as witnesses to the arrival of an extraordinary patient. An iron-mesh elevator door is pushed aside and we cram inside—two nurses and two guards from the prison. The elevator comes to a stop, and I am wheeled out into a hospital corridor. The gurney forges ahead, passing by white-clad nurses and the doors to rooms that are not prison cells. I'm in a hospital!

Through the haze of fear and uncertainty, I grasp that there is some kind of scenario here in which it is possible to function, at least for now. This has a profound effect on my ability to get a grip on my situation and to reorganize my thoughts. However, it is clear that there is still a very long and dark tunnel ahead. Waiting for me in the operating room is

Dr. Absalem. He doesn't say a single word to me. He is not nice. He gives orders, and I am transferred to the operating table. I look up at the medical team around me and suddenly all goes blank.

I awake in the morning and find myself in a hospital bed. There is no initial confusion. I know right away that I am a POW in Egypt. I look around. The room is large. Enormous, in fact. My bed is the only one in the room. It is near the left wall, parallel to it, about three feet away. The right wall, which is quite far from me, has windows running its whole length. But when I try to pick myself up to get a glimpse of the view, I discover that my entire body is encased in a plaster cast. Not quite my entire body. My right arm, thank god, is still free. Both legs are inside a single trousers-shaped cast called a spica. The cast covering the uninjured left leg is joined to the cast around the right leg by a broad section of cast around my trunk that is meant to stabilize the fractured right thigh. My left arm is in a cast from my fingers to my shoulder and bent at a ninety-degree angle. Never in my life have I broken, or even sprained, an arm or a leg, but now I've gone and done it big-time. Three of my limbs are encased in plaster, plus I have a wide plaster belt around my waist, up to my navel, connecting the leg casts and starting to make me uncomfortable all over.

But even in this "slightly awkward" position, there is much to learn about my room. The door, a metal one with two sections that open in opposite directions, is on the far left side. The walls are totally bare, devoid of any identifying marks or even the smallest picture. In the far right corner are a table and two chairs. Two men in civilian attire are sitting there. They watch me from afar. Not moving. There is a nurse in the room. She walks towards me and suddenly my head is spinning.

I feel the thirst that follows anesthesia. The cast is suffocating me. I can't move my limbs and I am weak, weak, weak. I know that she is beside me and I ask for water in Arabic. She takes a tongue depressor with some moistened gauze rolled around it and places it in my mouth. I suck the water and ask for more. When will I ever be free of this vicious thirst that has been tormenting me for… how long already? I do the calculation in my head and know that I am starting my third day in Egypt.

The nurse speaks to me in English. She asks how I'm feeling. As I mumble a response, I sink into a kind of half-coma. I know there's no point in rushing. I feel awful.

I wake around noon. All I want is to drink and to get out of the cast. Now there are three women nurses in the room. One of them, the oldest, comes up to me and introduces herself as the nurse in charge. She wets my mouth again using the tongue depressor technique and tells me I'll be okay. The two guards who were sitting in the corner before are now standing near my bed and staring at me curiously. The two other nurses join the head nurse, shoo the security guards away and begin to bathe me and change my bed linens. I gradually come out of the post-anesthetic haze and start trying to learn more about this new place. I can't touch the food that is served to me.

I'm squirming uncomfortably in the cast all the time. It is still soft and also a little damp, and I can feel how my movements are causing it to crack. In the evening, Sayeed comes to see me in the hospital. He speaks admiringly of the wonderful medical care I've received, tells me the Egyptians are fulfilling their part of the deal that we made back at the prison and that I shouldn't forget my commitments. "An Israeli pilot doesn't lie," he reminds me with a smile.

In the cast around my right thigh the Egyptian doctors have left a window over the open wound where the bone was protruding. Every so often, a nurse opens the "window," cleans the wound, sprinkles sulfa powder on it and closes it. Despite the treatment, my fever rises at night and I know that I have an infection, probably because of the open wounds. I take advantage of the pills I need to swallow to drink as much water

as I can, hoping to somehow quench this terrible thirst that
has been with me ever since I fell into captivity.

When I open my eyes, there are two new security men and
different nurses, but the daily routine has begun to take shape.
Bathing and making the bed in the morning, attempts to feed
me that don't go very well, a visit from the doctors once a day,
and a cast that is steadily cracking.

Late in the evening I am taken back to the operating room.
I am escorted to the operating room by a gaggle of nurses,
including some who were not part of the group assigned to my
case. Word has apparently spread that there is an Israeli pilot
here and they all want to get a glimpse of the unusual guest.
My right hand is holding on to the part of the bed-frame above
my head as I am being rolled down the corridor. One of the
nurses lightly strokes my fingers, evidently unable to suppress
the urge to touch someone from a world that is remote and
alien to her. I can't help myself—and I swiftly open and close
my grip. The Egyptian nurse lets out a shriek and leaps back in
fright. Everyone laughs.

But the bed keeps moving forward and the nurse,
unfortunately, does not return to caress my fingers. When I
awake the following morning, I find that the broken cast has
been replaced, and now my new leg casts are connected by
a solid rod that keeps them set apart and prevents me from
moving them and thereby cracking the cast again. The plaster
is still a bit damp, and a small two-legged heater is set up above
it to speed the drying process.

I have yet to form much of a relationship with any of the
shift nurses. There are eight of them all together, and two or
three work each shift. I am focused on my pain and discomfort,
on adjusting to an immobile life in my plaster prison, on my
fever that keeps rising each evening and not going down again
until morning, and on the attempt to figure out what rules of
conduct I should follow.

The security detail also consists of four pairs that relieve one another over the course of each twenty-four hour period. Some of the guards just observe me from their corner, others approach me and try to speak with me. I still can't eat. My metabolism is all messed up, and this only makes me feel worse and forces me to lie there in bed doing nothing.

The main thing that catches my attention so far is the way I am treated by the various people around. Ali, one of the guards, sits down next to me and tells me that he's not budging from my bedside until I eat lunch. He explains how important eating is for getting well, cuts the meat into little pieces and peels an orange and separates the slices. Another one, whose name I don't remember, never misses an opportunity to harass me. When he finishes eating in his corner, he comes over to me, puts his head next to mine and lets out a huge belch right in my face. When he is asked to empty my bedpan, he picks it up at an angle and spills half the contents over my groin, wetting a large portion of the sheet and mattress too.

The variations in the guards' demeanor and apparent social class are also fairly striking, but to me they are classified solely in terms of their attitude toward me. And this ranges from the hostility of the urine-spiller to the compassion of one, a student it seems, for whom this is a part-time job, who one evening slips a square of chocolate under my blanket.

Relations with the nurses are a lot more complex. Maybe because their routine involves caring for me on the most intimate level. They bathe me, treat the open wound in my thigh, help me turn on my side when they change the linens each morning and every evening to help prevent bedsores, massage my back with alcohol and sprinkle talc on my skin.

They too, though, can be classified on a similar spectrum ranging from outright hostility to genuine affection. One of them, Aisha, takes a special interest in me. She tries to arrange her shifts so that she'll be the one to massage my back each evening. This does not escape the notice of the security men, and one evening the more brutish ones try to physically block her from entering my room at a late hour when I am alone. But she stands her ground and makes her way past them. She comes to me, helps me roll over on my left side and gently tends to me while, as usual, she speaks to me in English about my condition and tries to understand more about me.

The head nurse engages me in conversation once in a while. I thank her for the nurses' care and say that I hope one day I can repay her with hospitality in Israel.

"Why do you say that?" she responds. "You know that the moment I get off the plane at the Lod Airport, the people there will hack me to death with their knives."

This is one of those moments that makes me think of the steep price exacted by all the boundless misconceptions—on both sides apparently—a price that is paid, in the end, by the people who are physically involved in the conflict. I express astonishment at her words, but she dismisses me with a wave of her hand as if to say, "You know that's exactly what will happen."

On the seventh day of my hospital stay, at about nine in the evening, the door opens and Sayeed enters with another man who looks to be about fifty. Like many of the Egyptians I've seen up to now, this man is wearing an untucked shirt that fastens with large buttons down the front and has two big pockets near the bottom. Following right behind them are two soldiers who are carrying a small table, which they place beside my bed. Sayeed and his companion ask how I am, and Sayeed adds that they believe that in my present condition we can now move ahead with our agreement—i.e., begin the questioning. My heart pounds wildly. I know I don't have much choice, but still I'm coming to a point at which I'm about to answer the Egyptians' questions without having been subjected to any physical pressure on their part in the last days.

The interrogator, who does not identify himself by name, orders a cup of tea and asks me if I would also like to drink. My instinct is to refuse. Answering interrogators' questions while drinking tea doesn't seem like respectable behavior for an air force officer. But from the second interrogation on I will completely change my way of thinking and switch from using the logic of a well-mannered Boy Scout to that of a POW in an enemy country—meaning, whenever they offer you something—take it and even ask for more. The nurses and security guards are far from my bed, and it's just the three of us around the table. I am in my bed, and the interrogator and Sayeed are on the other side of the table. Over the last seven days since I arrived at the hospital, I have tried to construct for myself a false world that will be strong enough to hold up under interrogation.

This world stands on two legs. The first leg of the story is that I am a reservist pilot in the air force. I fly very seldom, I belong to a squadron assigned to defend Tel Aviv, and so most of my flights are patrols between Tel Aviv and Netanya. The second leg is that I am a pilot whose squadron is stationed at the IAF airport in Herzliya. I remember from documents captured in the Six Day War that the Egyptians believed the Israeli Air Force had more airports than was actually the case. One of these was the airfield in Herzliya, which at the time was already a civilian airport for light aircraft. I have no idea whether it will be possible to build a stable enough story that rests on two such flimsy legs, but that is what I am setting out to do.

I give myself freedom to create an imaginary world. What worries me the most is whether I'll be able to give the same answers to questions I've already been asked, should they be repeated in the evenings to come. I have to invent a completely different routine of squadron life from what it is really like in the air force, so I can explain why I know only a few of the other pilots. It's incredible how captive we are to our routines—each little deviation from it feels like a transparent lie that will be immediately exposed. But no, sitting opposite you is someone who is not always equipped with information that can refute your story, and the reality conjured by your imagination becomes the real picture of the world.

To my surprise, as the evening wears on, I notice that while I'm engaged in constructing this false world, I am starting to relax a bit. The interrogator insists, for example, on getting the names of the pilots in the squadron. As a child, I lived in a Tel Aviv apartment building that had two entrances. In those days, in buildings like that, everybody knew everybody. And so, all the neighbors from Entrance A receive the rank of captain, and all the neighbors from Entrance B receive the rank of first lieutenant. And thus the 118th Squadron, a number that didn't exist then in the air force, is born. The interrogation lasts about three hours, until the interrogator finally stands up and promises to return the next day. I can't fall asleep for a long time after they leave. The thought that the next stage of my captivity has begun, the interrogations stage, inevitable as it may have been, jolts me into a new state of mind.

In the morning, when the nurses come to change my linens and serve me breakfast, I wonder if they know that I was questioned during the night nurses' shift and what they think about it, but their behavior is no different. They show no sign of knowing anything and go about their routines as usual. I wait with a pounding heart for the evening to come, going over and over my story from the night before, but Sayeed and the interrogator do not return.

That day, a man I didn't know had come to see me—I'd received a number of such visits from various intelligence officers—and asked if I needed anything. I told him that I was a religious Jew and that I needed a siddur, the Jewish prayer book. That afternoon a siddur was brought to my room and took its place alongside the Chinese-made toothbrush on the bedside table.

A whole world is contained within the siddur, even for a non-religious Jew. In addition to the prayers there are entire chapters of Psalms, of Ethics of the Fathers, and other passages from Jewish literature that were added for reasons unknown to me. The encounter with written material in Hebrew is overwhelming and reading the siddur becomes my primary activity whenever my fever isn't too high.

The next day, again at a late hour, the door opens and Sayeed and the interrogator enter the room. This time I also order a cup of tea, and then I wait with bated breath to see if the interrogation will begin with them proclaiming me a liar, or if it will continue from the point where we left off the last time. Have they questioned Nissim about what I said the other day, and has he unwittingly completely refuted my story? No, I am not a liar. The airport in Herzliya is active, the squadron defends Tel Aviv, I work as a building contractor, and once a month, my flying partner and I show up two hours before takeoff for a private briefing on our patrol shift. I sketch the airfield, I outline the runway, the route for vehicles, the squadron building, the hangar, the area where the planes park—and the whole time I am asking myself how long this story will hold up. The matter of my being a reservist pilot is put to the test when my interrogator extracts from his file a copy of my pay stub, the one found by the villagers, translated into Arabic.

Here I need to come up with a lot of accounting wizardry to explain the payment system for reservists. I am even called upon to explain the line on the pay stub that says one lira has been deducted for "the officers' club at the Hatzerim base" (where I served for two and a half years, up until three months ago), and it's quite amazing how one can come up with explanations for such esoteric things. I remind the interrogator and Sayeed that a meeting with the Red Cross representative is part of our agreement. The interrogator hastens to reply that the Red Cross representative will come, but only after the interrogation here is finished.

"How many questions do you have?" I ask. And he says, "Maybe another hundred, hundred and fifty."

Throughout the evening I am barraged with questions, and I maneuver between "I don't know" and fairy tales of my invention. At the end of the night, when the interrogator gets up, I tell him that I was counting the questions over the course of the night and that he passed the one hundred and thirty mark long ago.

"I understand that you are satisfied with my cooperation and now I expect to see the Red Cross representative," I add.

But the interrogator responds dismissively, "We still have a long way to go, we've barely begun."

"I will answer twenty more questions, and then I want to see the Red Cross."

Sayeed intervenes and tells me that I don't know what I'm talking about. "In Egypt, we don't count questions." I tell him that I expect the integrity I am showing as a military man to be duly reciprocated by the Egyptian military. They turn their backs on me and leave.

From time to time someone comes into my room—it's always a different person and I surmise that they are Egyptian intelligence officers who've obtained permission to do so in order to get an up-close look at this unusual creature that has arrived from Israel. They do not try to extract information from me but merely make conversation, mostly out of curiosity. The only way I can try to balance out the asymmetry between us is to ask, "Where were you in the Six Day War?"—what the Egyptians call the War of '67. Most of the visitors give evasive answers. None say that they were in combat. It's obvious that they served in various roles in intelligence headquarters here in Cairo. One surprises me with an unexpected response.

"I wasn't alive at the time." I gape at him in wonder, not grasping what he means to say. "I've erased those days from the calendar and from my life history. They're not a part of me." He becomes tense and I don't know what to say, and our easygoing conversation abruptly fades into an oppressive silence. He gets up and leaves.

I don't know how Sayeed and my interrogator will take what I've told them. Is there any opening for negotiation here? What is the next step? One thing about being in captivity all alone is that you have no one to consult with. And you have no way to develop other channels of information. Not only through friendly fellow prisoners you might talk with, but even merely through reading the look in someone's eyes or eavesdropping on other people's conversations. Having to lie here completely immobilized only compounds my helplessness and isolation.

Two days later, late in the evening, the door opens and Sayeed and the interrogator enter once more. They come over to my bed as if nothing special happened at our last meeting. "Where is the Red Cross representative?" I ask, sounding like I was certain that they would be bringing him along.

"After we're satisfied," says Sayeed.

"I'm ready to talk, but only after I see the Red Cross." The interrogator gets up from his chair, puts on the most serious expression he can muster, and says, "You won't answer the questions?"

"I told you—integrity for integrity." They turn around and exit the room. This isn't funny anymore, I tell myself.

After about five minutes the door opens, a soldier comes in—*Where do they come from so fast, all these soldiers?* —comes over to the bed and removes the siddur from the bedside table. I get nervous. I realize that I am leading myself down a hard road, but I have no choice. The idea that I've been communicating with my captors, two nights in a row, without having been subjected to any physical pressure, gives me no rest.

Even if I've lied nonstop. Even if I've constructed an imaginary world. The mere notion that such a dialogue took place, and while I was sipping tea no less, makes me very agitated. Though it's ridiculous to think that if I was badly beaten and then I talked, things would look any better. Still, what is happening does not match the captivity scenarios that I've had in my head for years. The seemingly decent medical care, the non-threatening daily routine, the occasional displays of kindness—none of this justifies deviating from what I've been taught about not giving information to the enemy.

And now here I am leading myself into the next stage.

I can't fall asleep. I don't know what I will see the next time the door opens. I am pretty sure I'll be returning to the prison, but it's all really just baseless speculation. I nod off at dawn and again the nurses wake me when they come to change my linens. The thoughts running through my brain give me no respite. What happens when you're in the prison cell and you suffer a kind of pain for which there are no outward signs? What if it's a toothache? What if, god forbid, a kidney stone? Who's going to pay any attention to such a complaint if the cause cannot be seen? What happens when, in addition to being in jail you are also encased in a plaster prison? My eye comes to rest on my toes that are sticking out from the casts on my legs. What happens if I get an ingrown toenail that eats into the flesh?

Nadia is one of the eight nurses caring for me, and the most impressive of them all. She has an upright bearing and is half a head taller than all the others, and also has a much lighter complexion. She attributes the latter to her Turkish parentage—her family is Muslim but not Arab in the ethnic sense of the term. She has a good command of English. She always wears a black brassiere whose color shows through the white of her uniform. Her behavior towards me is always correct and pleasant. She never shows any feelings of closeness like Aisha, but neither does she ever seem the least bit reluctant to tend to me, as is the case with some of the other nurses who are clearly not at all fond of me. Her body language and gestures project just what is needed to create a kind of mutual respect. With her erectness and proud bearing, she encapsulates the way I see myself—all I ever thought I was and all I hope to be in the course of this difficult experience, most of which still lies ahead. Our conversations often spill over into the personal arena. She wants to understand what an Israeli is and what sort of life I have back there, beyond the mountains of darkness, and in return she tells me some things about herself, like the story of her parents' migration from Turkey to Egypt, and her thoughts about wanting to become a doctor.

I call out to Nadia and tell her that one of my toenails is bothering me. She nods and continues with her work in the room. I assume that she regards what I said as just a bit of nuisance with no medical justification. A half-hour later, the wings of the door swing open and from afar I see Nadia entering and wheeling in a large metal treatment cart. She comes to the foot of the bed, rolls back the blanket, moistens a piece of cotton wool with alcohol and begins swabbing my toes. As I'm still lying there in disbelief, she takes a small scissors and, very carefully and attentively, starts trimming my big toenail. When she is finished, and satisfied with the state of the toenail, she squeezes some Vaseline from a tube and massages the nail and the toe. Without stopping, she takes the next toe between her fingers and begins clipping the nail. Her expression is serious, and she is absorbed in her task as if it were an advanced medical procedure. I lay in the bed, unable to take my eyes off her, amid a scene of a kind that was never discussed in the captivity briefings. I am acutely cognizant that at this moment, before my imminent transfer to the prison and all that will come in its wake—I am receiving a pedicure from a handsome Egyptian woman who I most likely will never see again in order to thank her.

When she finishes with the right foot, she turns to me and asks if what she has done thus far is satisfactory. I can't manage to say a word. I just nod and think about what is happening now back in Israel. I guess this is a reflex meant to counterbalance the strange scene unfolding right now just six feet from my eyes, which is turning this whole captivity experience into one giant seesaw. Nadia is focused now on my left foot. She finishes her work, collects all the instruments she used and places them in a small bowl on the cart, covers my feet with the blanket again, looks me deep in the eye for a long moment and then turns and walks away without saying a word.

Evening is approaching and there hasn't been much hustle and bustle in the room. My dinner is brought to me as a matter of course. On the tray there are no more pills for me to swallow. It seems that as far as the hospital is concerned I've completed my recovery period, although there is still a long orthopedic recovery period ahead until my broken bones heal. Only two guards are left in the room. They sit in their corner, smoking, reading the paper and chatting quietly.

Around midnight the broad doors of the room open wide. Sayeed is the first to come in, looking rather grim and not smiling at all. He is followed by four soldiers with a folded gurney. They come over to my bed, open up the gurney, lift me out of the bed that has served me faithfully for the past twelve days and place me on the rolling bed. Not a word is spoken. Sayeed doesn't venture to start any kind of conversation, and I already know to avoid asking questions that invite unpleasant answers. We go out of the room into the corridor and take the elevator down to the hospital lobby.

The air in the lobby is completely different. It is air that has come in from outside, from the street; it is the air of free people. Not warmed, not chilled, just air that means nothing special to a regular person walking down the street. For me it is an encounter with the normal world, with random people, with the ordinariness of a waning day. But the encounter is over in a flash. One of the soldiers takes out a cloth and quickly blindfolds me as the gurney continues its journey out the main door to the waiting minibus.

By now I've somewhat mastered the partial vision of the blindfolded. The general idea is to slide up the bottom part of the cloth that covers the tip of the nose. Success in doing so opens up two relatively unobstructed shafts looking down either side of the nose. Then all you have to do is to play with the angle of the neck, tilt it backward mostly, in order to see. Lying on my back on the mattress that has been placed on the floor of the minibus, every so often I sigh and scratch my face, and each time I surreptitiously push the fabric a little bit higher on my nose. Looking up and to the sides through the windows of the minibus, I see the half-darkened houses of Cairo, and the whole time I am silently bidding farewell to the hospital, to Aisha, to Doctor Absalem and especially to Nadia, as I head into the unknown.

Nine

25-SEP-1969

As I'm removed from the minibus and my next journey begins, I can tell that I'm being taken back to solitary confinement. The path followed by the stretcher, the turn into the narrow hallway, the complicated maneuvers from the hallway into the cell—I recognize it all from the last time. When the stretcher is placed on the floor, I rip off the blindfold. The cell is lit with the single bulb, a soldier I haven't seen before is spreading a sheet over the elevated bit of concrete that's standing in for a bed... before I can take in any more, I am lifted up by the soldiers and placed atop the sheet. The unfamiliar soldier silently continues with his work—covering me with another sheet and putting a folded sheet under my head. Meanwhile, the soldiers who escorted me here from the hospital fold up the stretcher and leave the cramped cell without giving me another glance. Now it's just me and the new soldier.

He is dark and handsome. His fingers are long and slender and his eyes are kind. He introduces himself and says his name is Sami. First in Arabic and then, when I explain that I don't speak Arabic, in very broken English. In the brightly lit cell I can see small bugs coming out of little holes in the walls and making their way up the sheet to where they can crawl inside the cast. I point at the bugs. Sami leaves the cell and comes back with a can of kerosene and a rag. He dips the rag in the kerosene and smears it over all the holes in the wall in an attempt to kill the bugs and to "upgrade" the cell's appearance.

The distance between my lower legs is wider than the bed. My left leg is suspended in air and my calf muscle is starting to ache. I can't close my legs because of the metal rod keeping the plaster casts fixed in place, and now it occurs to me that the Hebrew saying "Change your place, change your luck" can also have a negative interpretation. I point out to Sami my foot that is stuck in the air. He goes out again, and to my surprise, returns with a chair. He sets the chair next to the bed and rests my heel upon it.

I think now that the check-in process is complete, Sami will go and leave me alone. But no, he sits down on the chair and asks me who I am. I tell him that I am an Israeli pilot and that I have been in this cell before. He smiles and says that now he knows. With two fingers he mimes a bandage above the left eye. There is no trace anymore of the cut I had on the day I arrived.

"How do you know?" I ask.

"I saw a picture," he answers. My heart pounds. *Sami has seen a picture of me. In the newspaper, apparently. One of those that were taken on my first day in the prison. They know about me. They know I'm alive. What a relief!* At the hospital, the interrogator had told me that news of my captivity had not been publicized, and that cooperation on my part would make this happen faster, while non-cooperation would leave them with options I would have cause to regret. Patently false as this crude threat may have been, it had really gotten to me. That's what happens, apparently, when you're completely cut off from the world. And now Sami, in his attempt to create some communication between us, has given me almost full confidence that my plight is known. Not that I think the Israeli military knows exactly where I am at this moment, but still I try to milk this piece of good news for all it's worth.

"My brother was killed in the '67 War," Sami tells me.

"I'm sorry," I reply. "In war people are killed."

"Yes," he says, "but you shot him in the back when he was heading back to Egypt."

"I'm sorry," I say again. It sounds like I'm sorry for what happened to his brother, but really I'm sorry that out of all the jailers in Egypt, I had to get one who thinks we shot his brother in the back. I don't ask myself how he knows the details of the incident in which his brother was killed. That doesn't matter. What matters is this encounter once more with people who personally bear the scars of the conflict between Israel and Egypt. But Sami doesn't seem to hold a personal grudge against me for his brother's death. Despite his very poor English, he is relaxed and confident as he tries to speak with me, using hand gestures to make himself understood, and I gladly respond. I haven't yet experienced many consecutive days in solitary, but I can already appreciate the benefits of casual conversation with someone.

The conversation goes on for quite awhile, largely due to the language limitations. Sami keeps steering the discussion into politics. Like so many of the Egyptians, he too cites the map at the Knesset entrance showing Israel stretching from the Nile to the Euphrates as proof of Israel's expansionist nature and true objective in the Middle East. My vehement denials of the existence of any such map are received with much skepticism.

Sami persists, "And what about the Belfoor Declaration?" He says this in a triumphant singsong inflection that starts up high, swoops down low and comes back up so that the question culminates on the same note at which it began. His pronunciation throws me for a moment and I have to ask to make sure that Sami is indeed referring to "our" Balfour Declaration. I look at Sami, an Egyptian soldier serving as a guard at a Cairo prison, someone who clearly doesn't come from the elite ranks of Egyptian youth, and yet he not only knows about the 1917 Balfour Declaration that put forth Palestine as a place for the Jewish State but where to insert it in a discussion about the reasons for Israel's existence in the Middle East.

At three in the morning, without having resolved Israeli-Egyptian relations but having begun to establish our relationship, Sami says he is going to bed. He leaves the cell and locks it, and then I hear his footsteps fading away down the corridor. The light bulb over my head is still on. I close my eyes and try to fall asleep, still unsure just what the rules of the game are for an injured Israeli pilot who's unwilling to talk and has been placed in solitary confinement.

When I wake, for a moment I don't know where I am.

It's still early morning but already it's getting hot in the cell. I'm stuck in my plaster suit, no longer in my bed in the hospital in Cairo but here on this concrete slab. Above me is the asbestos ceiling with the lone bulb in the center, the light still blazing since when I nodded off. Behind me to the left is the cell door with the little window for the guards to peek through. In front of me and high up on the wall, just below the asbestos ceiling, is a window that faces out onto a yard of some kind, but it is almost completely covered by a nailed-on wooden board.

The door opens and a guard I haven't seen before comes in. He is shorter and heftier than Sami, and running across his very dark cheek is a scar of the type that you see on kids who have fallen on something sharp and jagged. He does not smile like Sami. He places a tin tray atop my cast—it's my breakfast, *aysh we-gebna*. Pita bread and white cheese. I scoot myself back a little, rest my head against the wall, pick up the pita and see that it is speckled with tiny ants. They must have been part of the flour. I take a bite of the cheese. It is very salty, but this cheese and this pita are the only items of food to be seen, no matter how far I look. The cheese has made me thirsty. I ask for water.

Othman, this is the guard's name, leaves and returns with a mug of water. I eat in silence as Othman watches me. I would rather not be watched like this while I'm eating, but I'm hardly the master of my surroundings at this point.

I'm feeling quite concerned about how to re-establish my standing as an officer in this situation, so it will be crystal clear to both him and me. This will be a key question throughout my captivity. There is no other role that I can take on—not the fool, or the befuddled soul, or the cool, laid-back fellow, or the meek and submissive one. Not the new admirer of the Egyptian republic. Up until two weeks ago, I was—I still am—an officer in the Israeli Air Force, and I realize that I will have to do what I can to preserve this image of myself. First of all, I mustn't show any signs of distress, as a general rule and especially not in front of the guards. Othman keeps his eyes trained on me. I finish eating and indicate to him that I need to do my business. Othman goes and brings a container similar to what I used in the hospital. For the urine he brings an empty can of tinned corn without a lid. I see that this is going to be a rather complex relationship. These men are prison guards and might be called upon to carry out harsh orders, yet meanwhile they have to tend to my hygiene as if they were hospital nurses. I wonder if they are going to exploit all my vulnerable points, or if they will draw a demarcation between different kinds of pressure tactics.

For the first time in my life, I have no one to consult with about something that's worrying me. And if Sayeed were to walk in right now, just asking the question would show weakness on my part, and seeking out each other's weaknesses is the very essence of our whole relationship.

Just as I'm thinking this, the door opens and there is Sayeed. There's tension in the air. Over the last two weeks I've made it a point to keep stressing that I am a captain in the Israeli Air Force, and Sayeed, whose rank I don't know but which I am certain is lower than mine, always treated me with respect in our meetings at the hospital. Now I've been thrown into solitary confinement, like the lowliest of prisoners, and this new situation means Sayeed has to construct a new relationship with me. It's clear to us both, mainly to me, that we are meant to be a couple, and this relationship will evidently have a major impact on what kind of life I am to lead in captivity—duration unknown, of course.

He orders Othman to leave the cell and is very harsh and unsmiling when he speaks to me. He wants to know if I've got the idea now and if I still insist on not talking. I repeat my stance—which I'm aware will not hold water much longer—that I've told them everything I know and that I want to see the Red Cross representative. Sayeed doesn't even bother to answer me. The wooden door closes, the key turns in the lock. I'm all alone again.

At noon, lunch arrives. Pita and cheese again, plus a piece of meat. The meat is a weird color. Purplish. One part of the meat is imprinted with the seal of the supplier. I can't touch it. It's getting warm in the cell and my eyelids grow heavy.

My dreams take me to Hatzor Airbase. I'm on the porch of the 105th Squadron building. Busy pilots are striding back and forth, talking to each other, putting on and taking off flight gear. I'm leaning on the iron railing and somehow I can't manage to talk with anyone. I can't see the people's faces. Every so often I call to one of them and try to speak with him, but they're all quite preoccupied. Everyone passes me by and ignores me. I wake in a panic to the reality of the cell and feel like a rock has just fallen on my head. Nausea mixes with the awareness that I'm in deep trouble. The thought that every time I sleep I might dream about Israel only to awaken to this awful reality scares me to death.

I'm thirsty. I call out for Othman and he comes. I ask for water and he goes out and comes back with water in a mug. This calms me because I see that I can get as much water as I want and that, for now at least, withholding water is not on their list of pressure tactics. I ask for more water and he gives me another mug to drink.

The cell keeps getting hotter. The right wall is again turning into a radiator, diffusing into the cell the baking heat of the afternoon sun that has been beating on it all day. Koranic verses blare nonstop over the prison loudspeakers. Evening comes and I can hear the new guard shift taking over. The sergeant gives orders, locks clang open and closed and I'm beginning to make sense of all the outside sounds. I glean from them the basic elements of life here, to feel something of a clockwork rhythm and routine.

Quiet descends upon the cellblock in the evening. The endless songs of Umm Kulthum fill the air now, and no other sound is to be heard. In solitary the twilight hours are the hardest. They have a special quality to them that reminds you that everyone else is finishing their workday and getting ready to go home and relax. I remember the same gloomy feeling from the sunset hours when I was on standby intercept duty at the Refidim base in Sinai. Tel Aviv and the family quarters at the base, with all they symbolized, were far away as we four pilots gathered in the standby building with the strange feeling that real life was happening somewhere else.

I feel that very same twilight sadness returning here, wrapped up in the jumble of emotions about captivity. I try to predict where things are heading to figure out how much longer I'll be in this place, but I haven't a shred of anything solid to cling to. Sami brings in my dinner—pita and cheese again and a cup of water—and disappears without saying a word. I grasp that he has taken over for Othman and feel glad that some kind of regularity is starting to take shape in my life. I fall asleep at night.

In the morning I awake into the void. I feel like the cell is gradually suffocating me. Deep down I want to believe that solitary confinement will only be a brief interlude designed to get a point across. And then I'll be taken back to the hospital, to the familiar room with the windows overlooking Cairo, with the eight shift nurses and even the guards. That was my home and which I rightfully have coming to me because of my injuries. But it's clear to me now that from here on this cell will be my home. That this is what I really have coming to me.

And solitary confinement is certainly living up to its reputation. Like the vermin trapped inside the ceiling above me, my mind races back and forth, back and forth over the same terrain. Each hour alone just increases its velocity.

I am isolated not only from the real world outside but also from my Egyptian captors. Our only connection revolves around feeding me and emptying my bowels. Occasionally, the door opens and Sami comes in with another jailer. He shows me to him, and they chat in Arabic and have a laugh together. I've become Sami and Othman's pet. This does not accord with my military seniority over them, and I do my best to ignore them whenever they enter the cell.

The days go by and the hopelessness and anxiety grow from day to day. I know how to function when I'm around other human beings. I don't know how to sink into absolute zero activity. Moreover, by ignoring me my captors are projecting a great deal of strength. They're not under any time pressure. They're not hurrying anywhere. As far as they're concerned, I can stay in this cramped cell for as long as I want. Uncertainty about the future steadily erodes your self-confidence. Where is the weekly program for the squadron? Where is the demanding schedule that appears on the bulletin board in the briefing room each and every morning? Where are the fines that must be paid to the squadron coffers by anyone who is late—by so much as a minute? I'm locked away in this isolated capsule and I'm the only person in the world who has no influence on anything whatsoever.

A fly is buzzing in the cell and I decide to catch it. I follow its movements and discover that it has an unvarying route. It keeps flying, over and over again, between four points: the center of the ceiling, the center of the left wall, the cast over my abdomen and the center of the right wall. Its flight path etches an imaginary and incredibly precise rectangle. The only chance of catching it is when it alights on my cast on its way to the right wall. It's a large fly and its buzzing is starting to bother me more and more, and all my attempts—at first to catch it alive, and then, after I've developed a deep personal hostility toward it, to kill it with one crushing blow—are unsuccessful. It just keeps relentlessly buzzing along its rectangular flight path. It has no way to get out of the cell unless Sami or Othman should show up and open the door. At long last it settles on the ceiling and rests there. For the first time, the thought strikes me that when a fly is standing on the ceiling it's really standing upside down. And this immediately sets my thoughts wandering to the world of upside-down flight and how, in time, it matters not to a pilot how he is flying in relation to the earth; from the limited viewpoint of the ground, it's all the same whether he is rightside-up or upside-down.

Will I ever fly again? It doesn't look like it. Amazing to think how early in my life this path that had everything I was looking for has come to an end. My thoughts meander.

The right wall starts to give off the afternoon heat once more. The fly is still standing on the ceiling, watching me apparently, and I am on the verge of finishing another day of being steadily reduced to a meaningless entity, to someone whose true weight in the world is dwindling down to nothing.

Ten

30-SEP-1969

The days chase one another. On the fifth day, the cell door opens and Sayeed appears—the non-smiling version. As usual, he is dressed in civilian attire—trousers and a casual shirt. He is different than all the others who come in contact with me and not only because he has no mustache. Somehow he always manages to convey the feeling of "I am a messenger."

He enters the cell and says he's come to see how I am. I tell him that I'm fine. He starts up a conversation, and I choose my words very carefully—so as not to look nervous and at the same time not to give the false impression that I'm enjoying myself and am pleased as punch to be in just this situation. He, too, does not express any extreme stance; he just wants to make certain it's clear who's sitting pretty right now and who's in an inferior position. He tells me that as soon as I wish to resume the interrogation, my situation will improve. I tell him that first I want to see the Red Cross representative. His expression turns grimmer than the conversation so far would warrant, and he explains firmly that since word of my capture has yet to be publicized and since they are still weighing their moves in regard to my fate, it is not possible to have me meet with the Red Cross. Convinced as I was that news of my captivity had already been made public, it is maddening to now find another shred of doubt gnawing away at me, and once again I am struck by my total isolation and disconnection from any trace of real information. I look him in the eye without saying anything. He turns and leaves the cell without a word.

As the days go by, the isolation and loneliness and idleness give way to fear. Fear of what? Fear of many things. Above all, fear of losing control of my actions. This is the fear that I'll find myself submitting to my interrogators and delivering to them the entire contents of my military mind. Fear not only that this is what will happen, but that it will happen when I am like a driven leaf, pleading for mercy, crying and wailing, a human dishrag. I am afraid of the way in which I will be brought to this terrible circumstance. First I will languish in solitary confinement for as long as they care to keep me here, and then the abuse will intensify and become physical and genuinely painful, and the sole part of my body that will be under my control will be my eyes, which I will be able to shift from observing one sphere of activity to another while being unable to stop any punishment from being inflicted anywhere upon me.

This fear that has taken hold inside me has a life of its own. Once the sequence starts running through my brain there's no stopping it. My breathing speeds up and I'm convinced that somewhere in Cairo people are sitting right now and planning out this very same scenario, except that for them it's the real thing, a plan to be put into effect. The narrow walls of the cell are closing in on me, and I wistfully imagine what it would be like to be free of the cast, to be able to move from side to side, to walk in circles, to do knee-bends and push-ups and everything a healthy prisoner can do even in a tiny room of just a few square feet. But in my condition I'm sentenced to a painful and endless stasis. I have to move my neck left and right every so often to keep the muscles from cramping, and I have to keep adjusting, with great difficulty, the position in which I'm lying in order to minimize the friction between my back and the cast, and between my back and the concrete bed, to prevent bed sores.

At long last I get a grip on the fear. I lie there flat on my back in the plaster cast, regulate my breathing, try to slow my perspiration and feel the strangely pleasant sensation of fatigue spreading through my body and leading me into sleep— oblivious to the heat, to Umm Kulthum who is singing and singing over the loudspeaker system, and even to Othman who comes in to take a peek. Just to sleep.

Eight days after being thrown into solitary the understanding truly dawns that I possess no ammunition. The hours keep passing, the blank walls have become oppressive and menacing, and a kind of black crust has formed on my body. The coating is most likely from the layers of sweat that dry on my skin every day after the western wall releases its heat into the cell. The cockroaches that Sami got rid of with the rag dipped in kerosene have begun to return. The light bulb in the cell burns day and night, the rats scurry overhead in the asbestos ceiling, and my head fills with the Koranic verses that are blared over the loudspeaker right on the other side of my cell wall. I've learned to wake myself when my dreams take me back to Israel, I've learned to adjust to the diet of ant-studded pitas, salty cheese and water, and I've even learned to get used to the idea of my jailers abusing me in various little ways related to tending to the needs of a person who's totally encased in plaster. But it's hard to get used to the fact that I am steadily shrinking into an inconsequential speck that has no clue as to what fate holds in store. Each day looks worse than the one before.

On the eighth day, at night, Sayeed comes into my cell once more.

I tell him that I'm ready to continue with the interrogation.

Eleven

04-OCT-1969

At midnight the cell door opens and I am taken to the next stop on my journey. When I remove the blindfold I see that I am in a big room. Not just bigger than the cell where I've spent the last eight days, but big in its own right. It is about twenty feet long and fifteen feet across. The bed is in the center of the room, and is extra high and wide. At the foot of the bed is a large desk with a broad chair behind it. There is a small bedside table to the right of the bed and the rest of the room is completely empty. It is very chilly. An air-conditioning unit affixed to the wall is going full blast and making the room freezing cold.

Sami is waiting for me in the room. He gives me a friendly smile and arranges my bed linens so I can lie there comfortably and be covered. I ask him to turn down the air conditioner. He tells me that this is how it is. It cannot be changed. I can see that it's an ordinary air conditioner and I try to explain to Sami about the two control switches, that one is for the temperature and the other is for the fan speed. After a few minutes in which I struggle unsuccessfully in the extremely limited Arabic I've acquired by now, to explain the workings of an air conditioner, he gets angry and tells me, "Here the air conditioners are not like the ones you have in your country. Maybe it will be taken care of tomorrow."

Instead he brings another blanket and puts it over me. I point out the blackness that covers my body. It has some light stripes in it. In solitary, I cleaned myself by scratching off the black layer with the nails of my right hand. This turned me into a human zebra because I couldn't make an even job of it. Sami exits through a door behind me and goes into an adjacent room, presumably the guards' lounge. He comes back with a towel soaked in warm water and starts wiping me off—first my face and then my right arm, my only exposed limb. Then he stops because the towel has turned completely black and is already useless.

This whole process made me feel like I was rejoining civilization. But I know there will be a price to pay, although I have no inkling yet as to what form it will take.

I revel in the comfort of the bed. After eight days on a concrete slab, my hair is stiff as iron, my body stinks and my beard is long and scraggly, but here I am on a normal bed again. Sami tells me that from now on I will have just two jailers. He will spend the nights with me and Othman will be with me during the day. I ask to see my face and from the next room he brings me a fragment of a mirror. I ask for them to shave me, like they shaved me in the hospital. Sami says I should think about keeping the mustache. A man needs a mustache. "You're a pilot and you need a mustache," he insists.

I have a long talk with myself about what it means that I am willing to be questioned again, and I don't drift off to sleep until nearly dawn. When I awake, Othman is in the room.

Breakfast is more elaborate than usual. On the tray is a blue plastic plate that holds, in addition to the pita and cheese, a puny tomato and a small dollop of jam. Next to the plate is a mug of tea, and this is the first hot—well, lukewarm, actually— drink I've had since the day I left the hospital. I expect that the questioning will resume in the evening and I am nervous in anticipation of the opening round.

Which Captain Giora Romm will show up at this interrogation? The one who was created since I fell into captivity? Or the real one?

This is my first opportunity to really communicate with Othman. He seems less intelligent than Sami; he's certainly less nice. His English is absolutely minimal, but seeing that I shall be in his company for as many days as I am to stay in this room, I need to figure him out and establish good communication between us. He takes away the breakfast tray and asks me if I am okay. I tell him that I want to continue getting cleaned up. He asks me by what name he should address me. I tell him that he should address me by my military rank—Captain. "*Na'am, ya kabtan*," he answers in Arabic. "Yes, Captain."

At the hospital, too, I was addressed as Captain, and I thought that of all the possibilities this is the best way to define myself, for as long as I can keep it up. Othman and I work on my hygiene for about two hours, and I feel like I'm preparing for the evening's questioning like a bride primping for her wedding.

Othman opens the main door to the room, which is in the wall to my left, and leaves. When the door swings open I catch a glimpse of a large courtyard outside. This is my first chance to reconnect with the world—a yard, gravel, the sun lighting up the space. The sight of the yard makes me feel like I've returned to Egypt from some remote exile on Devils Island. But then the door closes, and I'm left alone, imagining countless possible scenarios for the resumption of the interrogation.

What have they done in the interim? Have they tried to find out who I really am? Have they found out? The gap between who I really am and the character I've presented is large and worrisome...

After the Six Day War, I was the face of the Israeli Air Force. My name and picture appeared in every Israeli newspaper and in the international military press. My father enjoyed collecting newspaper articles that were sent to him from different Jewish communities around the world in every possible language. I'd downed five—three MiG-21s and two MiG-17s—enemy planes in aerial dogfights. In the lingo of fighter pilots the world over, a pilot who downs five planes earns the title of "ace."

I was the first Israeli ace.

Besides the fear that the Egyptians would see me as some kind of aviation "genius" and therefore expect to extract information that I did not possess, I worried that I would become a pawn in the propaganda war between the two countries—i.e., "Look at the great hero of the '67 War lying here useless in the hands of the Egyptian Air Force."

When the war began on June 4, 1967, nearly the entire Israeli Air Force had taken off to attack the Egyptian Air Force's airfields. Just twelve interceptors—two pairs of planes from each of the three Mirage Jet squadrons—remained on the ground to defend the nation. It was inevitable that Arab planes would come to counter our opening salvo. I was in the first pair.

When I entered the cockpit about an hour before the first takeoffs of the war, sat down in the pilot's seat and leaned forward so the ground crew could help me adjust the shoulder straps, I felt like I was carrying the entire population of Tel Aviv on my back. Two hours later, just as I was starting to chafe at being left out of one of the most important operations in Israeli Air Force history, my flight leader Eitan and I were ordered to take off for the Suez Canal area.

In two separate air battles over the Abu Sweir Airfield near the Suez Canal city of Ismailiya, I downed two MiG-21s. In the space of just ten minutes, I, Giora, who five years earlier was still in high school, had done the kind of thing I'd always associated with adventure stories or movie scenes. That same afternoon I flew northeast to Syria to attack a military airfield called T4 near the ancient desert city of Tadmor. There I downed my third MiG-21. In the evening, when the day's combat was done and I found myself alone, in my mind I was a whole new person. But then I learned what war truly is. Danny Angel, my close buddy from high school, also a pilot, was killed on the same day of my triumph. Now I understood that between these two points—perfect execution of a mission on the one hand, and precious loss of life on the other—was evidently where this animal called War was to be found.

Two days later, I downed two Egyptian MiG-17s over the Sinai Peninsula. And so, on the third day of the Six Day War, I became the Israeli Air Force's first-ever ace.

The stories were numerous and of the same kind. I was the embodiment of Israeli combat brilliance—i.e., a young Sabra, a product of the Israeli school system, a dedicated member of the Scouts youth movement, suddenly accomplishing feats previously only familiar from the books we'd all read about World War II like *The Battle of Britain*, *Spitfire Over Malta*, and *Tale of a True Man*. Ace fighter piloting were the kinds of acts that happened in distant foreign lands, at a time when European Jewry was being obliterated in the twentieth century's greatest atrocity. And now, just twenty years later, here's this young Israeli flying one of the world's top fighter planes, the French Mirage, and downing five Russian-made planes in aerial combat. *Russian* planes. The same planes that had terrified all of Israel along with its supporters around the world before the six day Israeli blitz. Diaspora Jewry foremost among them. Or some variation thereof.

Four of the planes I shot down were flown by Egyptians. What would my captors do with me if they found out my real identity? To have the symbol of Israeli aerial omnipotence in its custody, battered and immobile, would be a political windfall for Egypt. They could parade me around and torment my family. What was more weighing though was wondering how long I would be able to keep my secret.

When they questioned me at the hospital, I maintained that I was someone with a very modest military career. As for my participation in what they call "The '67 War," I've told them that my plane was hit on my first sortie, that I made an emergency landing at the Ramat David Air Force Base, that I was taken to the hospital in Afula in northern Israel and that I spent the remainder of the war there.

There were elements of truth in this, because a good lie needs some kind of real anchor. I had been hit on the second morning of the war, I had landed at Ramat David, and I had been taken, injured, to the hospital in Afula. But the next morning I ran away from the hospital, returned to my squadron at Tel Nof and during the only sortie I was able to fly at the end of that day, I downed those two more Egyptian planes near the Suez Canal.

The gap between who I really am and the character I've presented is large and worrisome. I expect that I will eventually pay a high price for it. In my isolation and in my never-ending discussions with myself, these anxieties have steadily progressed from an initial complacency to something verging on panic.

I don't want to go back to solitary!

The feeling of suffocation and nothingness of lying there in that cell is still with me, and I know that it's just a blindfold and a two-minute ride on a wobbly gurney away.

Twelve

04-OCT-1969

Othman comes in with lunch. It's obvious that the conditions provided by the Egyptians follow very specific guidelines. Lunch consists of cooked meat, cooked vegetables, a bowl of rice and an ant-speckled pita, cut in quarters. For dessert, there is a small orange.

All in all, things are looking up.

The hours pass slowly. At seven in the evening, Sami arrives, smiling, and addresses me as Captain. He sits down at the big desk in front of me and takes out his dinner. He's brought along from Cairo a meal of *ful*—cooked fava beans—wrapped in a cone of newspaper, and another paper cone full of *tushi*, the hot pickles that go with the ful. The two of us eat in silence; him his ful and me my dinner. After the meal Sami takes out a cigarette. He's a pretty heavy smoker, apparently. I start chatting with him about this and that, just to try to establish my desired formula for relations between us, a partnership for what look to be the long days ahead. A partnership between a captive and his guard, between a pilot and a jailer, between an officer and a simple soldier. My hope is that the attitude I've chosen to adopt will be taken as friendly, not condescending, and simultaneously give rise to a sense of respect for someone who is higher-ranking, albeit an enemy—all with the aim of trying to neutralize as far as possible my jailers' ability to humiliate me whenever the mood strikes them.

At ten at night, the door opens. Sayeed comes in with another man. For a moment the sight of him takes my breath away. He is red-haired, short, and with his mustache he looks like a perfect cross between Nissim Ashkenazi, the other Israeli POW, and King Hussein. I can't take my eyes off him until it finally sinks in that he is a person in his own right.

"This is Aziz," Sayeed says to me. "He will handle the talks with you from now on."

Not "will interrogate you," not "will question you," not "will beat the crap out of you if you don't give him everything he wants." He'll just "handle the talks from now on." A rather mild version of the reality, the more civilized depiction perhaps, intended to help me swallow the cooperation that is supposed to resume here.

Aziz projects a great deal of authority. He comes right over to the big desk, and without making any eye contact with me, sits down in the chair on the other side, places his leather briefcase on top and takes out a thick bundle of papers. These are the notes from my questioning up to now. He slowly arranges the pages on the desk, looks at Sami to his right and tells him to bring him an *ahwah mazbut*—the excellent coffee that is served on a small metal tray alongside a glass of cold water.

Sayeed says to bring him one too, and then I am asked if I would like something to drink. I ask for tea with lemon, not because I don't like coffee, but because at this stage I can pronounce *chai ma'a lamoun* with a good Egyptian accent and because by making a different selection I'm sending the message: *Here is someone with an independent and distinct personality.*

"We'll start from the beginning," says Aziz, straightening a stack of blank white papers before him and shifting the historic pile of papers to the right. My attempts to guess Aziz's plan don't stand a chance. His expression is stern and gives no reason to suspect that he likes me, even a bit. He does not project the relaxed attitude of *So, we have a long road ahead of us – Let's do this as efficiently as possible so we can all go home happy.*

Next to him, Sayeed looks smaller than ever.

The only thing I can imagine is that he is an air force intelligence officer, and that he has been assigned the project of Captain Giora Romm. I just hope that they haven't made his promotion dependent upon his success here. If I could've just found some more calm inside me, I might have remembered that Egyptian Air Force intelligence, according to data that even I was familiar with, couldn't find Mt. Everest unless it crashed into it. But in the big room in Abbasiya Prison in Cairo, Aziz is the king of the hill and I'm the designated sacrifice for the slaughter.

Aziz starts the questioning with my life story. The farther along we get, the more inquisitive he becomes, wanting to know every detail about my career path since the day I enlisted in the military.

Then a problem.

Two months before I fell into captivity, Miriam and I had taken a trip to the United States. I picked up a few slang phrases there, including the common exclamation "Oh boy."

Aziz didn't go to America with Miriam and he apparently isn't familiar with the expression. He takes the words literally and thinks that I am calling him a boy. I couldn't have made a bigger mistake on the night of our first meeting. You don't need an air conditioner in the room to feel the chill.

Meanwhile, I understand that this is just the prelude to the real interrogation and that Aziz is busy spreading traps to see which ones I will fall into later on. As the questioning proceeds, I am living in two worlds simultaneously: this external world in which I am giving slow and deliberate answers to each question and my internal world in which I am trying to etch into memory the tales I am busily inventing.

At around two in the morning, Aziz gathers up his papers and says we'll continue the next day. His exit is quick and charmless. Sayeed follows him out, and immediately afterwards, Sami, who has been sitting outside the whole time on the three steps that lead from the door to the yard, comes into the room.

Again I can't fall asleep. Aziz was of a different magnitude than the interrogator in the hospital. To be honest, he was scary mostly because I had the impression that he was one of those short people who have to compensate for it with an assumed toughness. I review in my mind my latest biography and all the other bits of information that I fabricated in the course of the interrogation. What I wouldn't give now for a pencil and paper! But the room is empty. Nothing here but me and my powers of recall.

Thirteen

05-OCT-1969

Aziz reappears at ten o'clock the next night, again with Sayeed. Again the *ahwah mazbut*. Again Sami sits outside on the steps.

But the really fascinating part is that I am still a reservist pilot in the Mirage squadron that fiercely defends Tel Aviv from its base in Herzliya. I take some comfort thinking that they do not yet know who I am. But now we have to get into the details. Names. Numbers. Aziz wants to hear about the flight on which I was hit.

"What was your call sign?" he asks.

"I was Fence Two," I answer him, reminiscing about my call sign from my first sortie in the Six Day War, the one in which I crossed the border for the first time in my life and downed my first two MiGs, not that far from where we are right now in fact. My call sign when I was hit was actually Tulip Four, and it really makes no difference if I tell the truth on this point or not, but the internal pressure to not utter even a single true word is increasing, and here I am inventing yet another false detail that I must now add to my life story.

Aziz keeps expanding on the subject until we are discussing the entire air force. Where are the air force squadrons located? Where is the control system deployed? How many pilots are there?

"I want to know everything," Aziz says intently, and I'm lying there across from him, thinking, "And I don't want you to know anything." It's after midnight now, and I ask for tea. With a dramatic flourish, Aziz holds his hands at eye level and claps three times.

One, two, three.

The door opens and Sami enters. He stands there submissively, awaiting orders. For a second I feel like I'm watching a play about Harun al-Rashid, the caliph from Baghdad. Sami is sent to fetch a round of drinks. Aziz does not let up. He wants to know all about the air force, and I persist in professing ignorance. I have no idea at what point in my maneuvering and evasiveness they'll apply the weapon of solitary confinement, but this interrogation is no laughing matter anymore.

It never was, actually, but now that I'm aware of what tactic the interrogator has at his disposal when faced with a recalcitrant POW, a tactic I experienced for eight days, I become tense and agitated. Every so often the insulting "Oh boy" escapes me, and I feel like I haven't yet found the magic formula for maintaining a cool exterior despite my inner turmoil.

The next morning, after the usual breakfast, it strikes me that the interrogation process, scary as it is, has a certain advantage to it. It is much preferable to the isolation and loneliness of solitary. If I can manage to lie so much, I must possess a certain amount of power. The major weak point is the moment when the lies will be exposed. What or who will protect me then? The punishment scenarios run through my head again. They do not end well from my point of view. Not one of them.

Aziz comes nearly every evening. At his request, a small table has been brought into the room and placed to the left of my bed. Now he interrogates me from a much closer distance, so that he can scan my body language as I am questioned, as I consider my answer and as I respond. Like in a poker game.

He has also softened a little. I can occasionally get a smile out of him, while Sayeed's boisterous laughter fills the whole room. Now we take a break in the questioning while Sami brings us our midnight beverage. At Aziz and Sayeed's urging, I now drink *ahwah mazbut* too. I allow myself to drift onto completely unrelated topics. I tell them about watching the Apollo 11 moon landing, which I experienced in New York. I make Sayeed swear that, POW or not, he must tell me when Apollo 12 is launched and when another successful moon landing is made.

But Aziz isn't interested in Apollo 12. He wants to know the numbers of the air force squadrons, the names of the pilots in the squadrons, all about the electronics systems in the Mirage and endless details about the air force and the IDF, to fill in all the holes in Egyptian intelligence's picture of things. Meanwhile, I feel like the whole weight of keeping the air force hidden from Egyptian intelligence is on my shoulders. The effort not to give away a single valuable piece of information feels like a tricky flight maneuver—nothing but perfect execution will do.

On a more practical level, the fear is continually simmering that a first small concession will quickly snowball into more. You give away just one reliable detail and before you know it, it's linked to another question and another question, and the threads of the painstakingly knit false garment will come unraveled in a flash. One evening I celebrate an important victory. I'm asked about the type of radar the air force has at Mitzpeh Ramon in the Negev, and for a change, this is something that, unlike dozens of other times, I honestly do not know the answer to. I say that I don't know. I'm accused of lying and after fifteen minutes I'm asked the same question again. This question comes up again and again. I don't know, and I'm on the receiving end of Aziz's growing anger. Towards the end of the evening I'm asked the same question yet again.

"I don't know!" I shout, with no warning. All the fatigue, tension and fear, and the relentless effort to preserve the safety and wellbeing of the air force, turn into a cry that bounces off the walls.

"I don't know, I don't know, I don't know!" Silence descends upon the room and Sayeed looks at me in shock. Up to this moment, he hasn't seen me lose my self-control or raise my voice. He and Aziz exchange glances, and the latter does not return to this question again. The next morning, when I go over in my mind the previous night's questioning as always, I note to myself that I have a bit of rope I can use with this "I don't know." This rope must be saved for important things.

How asymmetrical the struggle is between interrogator and subject, I think. The interrogator has pressure tactics at his disposal. Moreover, the subject has no idea what the interrogator knows from other sources. No way to know when he is asking a real question and when the question is designed solely to test the subject's veracity. And worst of all here, the thing that gives me no respite—what has he compared with the interrogations of Nissim who is surely being questioned in parallel with me and is unaware of my presence here?

The interrogator, however, cannot know what information the subject holds in his mind. So the interrogations soon become a riveting intellectual contest. And this confrontation also takes on a personal aspect as a consequence of the interaction between questioner and subject. But the thing that is uppermost in my mind at all times is this: In the end, if anyone has to go to solitary confinement, it will be me and not Aziz.

Fourteen

06-OCT-1969—12-OCT-1969

Life with Sami and Othman becomes closer as time passes. The days and nights that we share, the handling of my various needs, the conversations that become more and more personal—all this makes us closer. Sami is still my preferred guard. He's a big fan of Zamalek, Cairo's top soccer team, and we talk a lot about the wonders of the game. He is gentler, his smile is endearing. I feel that if the need arises to beat me, it will be Othman and not Sami who performs the task.

Once a week they come to shave me. The prison barber is a very short man. He has a brown leather suitcase from which he removes the shaving soap, the shaving brush and the crowning glory—the razor blade that he hones with swift and precise motions on a brown leather strop held taut between his clamped armpit and his left hand. He shaves me carefully so I won't get nicked. Yet I can't help but feel terrified every time he runs the blade along my neck, passing it over the windpipe.

Seeing Othman standing beside him throughout the shaving process doesn't make me feel any calmer. Finally he cleans my face with a towel and goes over it with an antiseptic stone. The stone, something that Israeli barbers stopped using a long time ago, arouses nostalgic feelings from when I was a little boy watching my father's morning shave. I remember that he also used just this kind of stone.

My father picked up and left behind his loving family in Warsaw, Poland when he was nineteen to set off for Israel. He did so because of the Zionist upbringing he received at home, at school and in the youth movement he belonged to, the Halutz movement in Poland. In a nutshell, this Zionist education taught that the Jewish people had to return to the piece of land to which God had led them and from which the Romans had exiled them thousands of years before. So he left his country, his home and his family at age nineteen and headed east.

Nineteen! To take total responsibility for your life at just nineteen? He made it to Israel, where he lived a hard life filled with frequent hunger, difficulty in finding work, and relentless pressure to pack it in and return to Europe as many of his comrades did (unwittingly dooming themselves to become part of the statistics of the Holocaust). My father refused to give up and go back to Poland.

He scraped and saved to purchase immigration permits to Palestine from the British Mandatory Government of those days. And seven years after leaving Poland, he brought all of his family to Israel—parents, brothers and sisters—and blessed them all with long and fruitful lives. This was the man who, growing up, I used to watch shave. And now, for the very first time, my mind made room for the thought that all the MiGs I downed and all the symbols and medals I wear on my uniform were meaningless next to the accomplishments of my father.

My mustache is getting quite bushy. I think it looks terrible but Othman pronounces his professional opinion of it, and to him it's a needed signifier of my masculinity, not to mention an accoutrement that reinforces the "captain" in me. Othman tries to impress me with his knowledge and every day, after breakfast, he carefully scrutinizes the morning paper at the big desk in my room. From extended observation of his motions, I conclude that he's not actually reading but merely performing a ritual of shifting from one page to the next, making sure to create the kind of rustling noise that generally accompanies the energetic perusal of a newspaper.

Nearly every day, with a joy tinged with gloating, he shows me the editorial cartoons in *Al Jumhuriya*, the Egyptian daily that the prison guards receive. They always feature Israeli elements, the caricatures distorted by anger and hatred, whether it's Golda Meir or Moshe Dayan or Israeli soldiers and so on. Othman laughs heartily when he shows me the daily cartoon. While I, with my ridiculous patriotism, get mad at the way that Israel is depicted in the pages of *Al Jumhuriya* and try to refute the cartoon's message, as if at that very moment Skyhawk and Phantom aircraft are not diving over the Suez Canal area and turning it into a wasteland.

When he really annoys me, this Othman, I talk loudly to him in Hebrew. I unleash everything that has built up inside me, and it unnerves him. He demands that I stop speaking Hebrew but I just increase the pace of my words and the loudness of my voice. Finally I calm down, lie back in the bed and try to figure out what will become of me. Where is all this going? I've been in captivity for over a month now. There is no sign of the Red Cross. What sort of country do I have that cannot force the Egyptians to comply with even such a basic thing?

I find myself thinking a lot about what is happening back home. Ironically, I find that I worry about my family all the time. Things can happen, after all, and the moment I imagine them happening, they become real in my mind. I picture a long series of possible accidents, explosions, illnesses and disasters, and my eyes fill with tears as if the figments of my imagination were becoming reality there far away.

At ten at night the door opens as usual and my heart pounds faster. There's a change. Instead of Aziz, in walks an Egyptian officer, with Sayeed trailing behind.

The new man is in a plain khaki uniform devoid of any kind of insignia. The uniform looks like it was just carefully pressed and is as crisp and distinguished as an officer's uniform could possibly be. The trouser legs are tucked into a pair of gleaming black boots of fine quality. The officer is quite tall and handsome. Everything about him says, "I am a pilot," before he even opens his mouth. Sayeed introduces him, "This is an Egyptian pilot. His name is Anwar."

Anwar sits down at the desk by my bed. He starts going through the, apparently inevitable, ritual for new interrogators—i.e., busying himself in a way that demonstrates who has the upper hand, emptying his briefcase and arranging his papers on the desk. I don't utter a word. This is the first Egyptian pilot I have ever laid eyes on. An impressive figure. Have I encountered him and his pilot comrades flying in their MiGs over the Sinai, above the Suez Canal, or in the desert south of Jabel Galala when we came in our Mirages? His body language says he belongs to the Egyptian elite. Sayeed sits far from him, farther away than he usually sits when Aziz is the interrogator.

Anwar lifts his gaze and aims it at me. "I've gone over the notes from all your interrogations. I've read them carefully. You never stop lying for a moment." He says this with the authority typical of one of our squadron commanders summing up the daily briefing in the squadron briefing room. I notice this right away but inside I am still in turmoil—still quite awed by this striking personage. His English is that of someone who was educated in the language. It is flawless. I am so sorry that this meeting is not taking place when I am in uniform, on an equal footing. I'm ashamed of my reduced condition, which broadcasts to both of us, "Look at me and look at you." What I would pay to be able to describe to him right now how I downed four Egyptian planes during the Six Day War. And then to casually remark at the end that I'm saving the story of how I downed the Syrian MiG-21 for when I have a chance to tell it to a Syrian colleague of his. But I must remain inside my minimalist shell, pretending that being a pilot is just a secondary occupation for me.

"About what, for instance?" I say to him, asking him to provide an example of my lies, and essentially trying to see if he is going to bring crashing down the whole tower that I have so arduously built up to this point.

"Twice you described the flight in which you were hit. One time you said that a siren was heard in the squadron, and then you ran to the plane. And another time, that a bell rang in the squadron, and then you ran to the plane."

Achieving credibility in captivity requires fantastic self-control. There can be no confusion. No stuttering. No "I made a mistake." An answer must be fired back to each question fired at you.

"In the squadron, for the sake of redundancy, there is both a bell and a siren. One time I mentioned the bell and the other time the siren. It's quite simple. Don't you have the same thing?" Or in other words—I am also curious about your world, and I am a pilot and therefore I can permit myself to behave as your equal.

"Here, I ask the questions." Anwar is older and more mature than me. At the time he was the commander of a MiG-21 squadron at the Egyptian airbase at Inshas, northeast of Cairo. He was killed four years later, in what his family surely refers to as the October War.

Fifteen

12-OCT-1969

Anwar asks about the Herzliya base and starts to go into details about life there. I see that this interests him. We talk about it. We go over the layout of the base, the regular schedule of squadron. And then, in a variation from what has been the practice up to now, the door opens and the hot drinks are brought in by Sami and by Anwar's servant.

"You see," I say, "we don't have soldier servants in the air force. We have a different attitude about officer-soldier relations."

"Is that so?" he answers me. "And the soldiers on mess duty who serve you food, isn't that another form of servant relations?"

I have no need to start an ideological debate here, so I let it pass. Anwar is very keen to know whether there are American pilots in the Israeli Air Force. He wants to know about the black boxes in the Mirage, which give us, he says, an edge over

the Egyptians in terms of electronics. But I know that what he
is really looking for is information about the Israeli Air Force's
ability to down planes in dogfights. He wants to hear about
aerial combat training. These are not the sort of questions that
require brief and precise answers. Here the respondent can be
free to indulge his powers of exaggeration and obfuscation, and
I provide superbly longwinded and hollow answers, deriving a
kind of pleasure from it.

At his request, I describe the flight in which I was hit.
Oddly, I feel a pang of humiliation when I cite the name of the
call sign I made up—Fence Two, rather than Tulip Four. I've
always been very fond of and remembered my call signs from
special flights. Painful as it is, Tulip Four is the call sign of the
flight from which I did not return.

Anwar wants to know about Tel Aviv's aerial defense
system. "I don't know," I reply. "I don't think we have any
special defense system for Tel Aviv."

"Yes you do," he insists. "Tel Aviv is the largest city in
Israel, the financial center. Tel Aviv is the capital of Israel. Tel
Aviv must have an air defense system."

Lying there in bed I am indignant. "Jerusalem is the capital
of Israel, not Tel Aviv."

"No, no," Anwar attacks. "Al Quds is not yours. It is an
Arab city. Tel Aviv is the capital."

"Jerusalem is the capital," I respond without hesitation.
"Our president is in Jerusalem. The Knesset is in Jerusalem.
The government is in Jerusalem. Jerusalem is the capital of
Israel." By nearly every conceivable parameter, the Six Day
War was a turning point for Israel. First and foremost, the war
established Israel's standing as the most powerful country in
the Middle East, stronger than any individual Arab nation as
well as all of them put together. As the deputy IDF Chief of
Staff from that war Lieutenant General Haim Bar-Lev put it,
Israel did so in a way that was "decisive, quick and elegant."

The war was preceded by a three-week period in which the Arab states, chiefly Gamal Abdel Nasser's Egypt, gradually closed in on Israel by massing large forces along the Egypt-Israel border, closing the Straits of Tiran (Israel's naval passageway to the south, the Red Sea and the Indian Ocean), and by forging a menacing military coalition along with Syria and additional forces dispatched from Arab states that have no border with Israel.

All this was accompanied by aggressive propaganda in all the media outlets of the time, propaganda that boiled down to a call for Israel's destruction once and for all. As a deep sense of dread overtook practically the entire nation, the Israeli military prepared one of the greatest military surprises of the twentieth century. When the war erupted, the Israeli Air Force, in the course of a single day of combat, wiped out the air forces of Egypt, Syria and Jordan, thereby making their ground forces on all three fronts exposed and vulnerable. Within six days, the three Arab countries were vanquished as Israel destroyed vast numbers of their forces and conquered territory four to five times its size, including Jerusalem.

The Six Day War reset the balance between Israel and its neighbors. Anwar must have missed the memo.

"Al Quds is not yours, and we will take it back," Anwar says firmly.

I turn my head toward Sayeed. "I am unwilling to continue the interrogation if Jerusalem is not the capital of Israel."

Anwar fires right back, "Don't make us treat you differently. We can do that." The atmosphere in the room changes all at once.

"Jerusalem is the capital of Israel," I say and lay my head back on the pillow. A situation has arisen that none of us anticipated. A half-minute of silence ensues in which it is clear to all that the interrogation has deviated from any kind of reasonable script. What now? How do we get out of it?

"Gentlemen," Sayeed interjects, "You are pilots, you are officers, you are fighters. You are not supposed to get into politics. Please, continue with the matter at hand."

Did he just call me a gentleman? Here in Abbasiya Prison? A gentleman? Me? With my plaster casing and this idiotic mustache?

Anwar and I look one another in the eye, trying to gauge what the optimal maneuver is at this moment. Anwar accepts Sayeed's suggestion, and we both immediately embrace the ladder that Sayeed has proffered to us and climb down from the tree.

Anwar continues questioning me until three in the morning. When he gets up to leave, I feel great sorrow. Since I've been in captivity, he is the first person who has made me feel true awe.

The interrogations continue but Anwar gives the mantle back to Aziz. Now they are held every two or three days, always between ten at night and three or four in the morning. I feel my nerves gradually coming undone.

Here and there some inconsistencies have come up. Each time that Aziz enters my room, I need five minutes for my body to get a grip on the turmoil raging within me and on the nerves and the fear that perhaps tonight he is coming with information that will knock down everything I have built up to the night before. I feel that I cannot keep on tossing up and juggling so many balls of lies that soon they will start to drop on the floor. And then, in one interrogation session, when Aziz gets up to leave, I tell him that I have now spilled everything that I know. I request to meet with a Red Cross representative. Aziz looks at me with scorn. And then, in a burst of anger, I tell him that there is no point in him coming back to this room anymore. I have said all I have to say.

It is two in the morning.

At three, I'm back in solitary confinement.

Sixteen

20-OCT-1969

It is morning. The cell door opens. Othman, arriving for the day shift, is standing there.

"*Kedha kwayis, ya kalb*," he says with a nasty thin-lipped smile that bares his upper teeth. Like, "This is fine, you dog." He scans the tiny cell like a general surveying a vast battlefield. Upon finishing, he looks at me threateningly and leaves. I hear the jangling of keys and the sound of his footsteps fading away.

I am dumbfounded. Othman. Our Othman. The simple jailer who for the last month I've trained to address me by my rank, to see to my hygiene needs, to not dare tell me a dirty joke, which he tried to do one day. Othman. What a radical shift in our relationship. Up until yesterday, when he left in the evening, it was, "As you wish, Captain," and, "Just a moment, Captain"—and now it's *ya kalb*.

And most upsetting of all is how upset this makes me. I wonder what Sami will be like when he comes tonight. The last time I saw him, he accompanied the guards who transferred me back to solitary, spread out a sheet for me to lie upon, placed a folded sheet under my head, covered my naked body with another sheet and left without further ado.

But my real worry, of course, is what turn my relations with Egyptian Air Force intelligence will take now. My whole time in captivity, in my mind at least, can be summed up in two words—loneliness and fear. Fear and loneliness. And there is no way to truly explain what they mean to anyone who hasn't experienced them in their raw form. In their most violent form.

The counterweight to them is another pair of words—courage and self-control. The necessity, and the capacity, to bridge between the inner experience of fear and loneliness and an outward show of self-control that draws on reserves of courage is experienced as an actual physical sensation of the nervous system. The feeling that your nerve endings are about to be shredded by the awful tension that is a constant in this life of total uncertainty, a life in which you have only the slightest ability to shape the course of events. The skin of my hands had begun to peel and crack before I was returned to solitary confinement, and now sores are also developing on my scalp.

How will the interrogation continue now? After all, it's most unlikely that Aziz will suddenly show up in the cell and say, "Listen, you're right, here's the phone number of that Red Cross fellow, let's give him a call." So what will restart the engine of our relationship? I lie here in the cell with the songs of Umm Kulthum ringing in my ears, seething with anger at the State of Israel. In a fury, I pick up a dry pita left over from the morning's *aysh we-gebna*, turn towards the right wall and start to scratch a message into it.

The top line is, "They know about you. They'll get you home." And below it, "It'll be okay."

I lie back on my back.

A few minutes later I turn my head to the right... whoa, what's written here on the wall?

"They know about you. They'll get you home. It'll be okay."

A feeling of calm slowly spreads through me. I lie flat on my back now, staring up at the ceiling like a corpse in the city morgue, letting the night fill my cell and overshadow the eternally lit bulb.

Inwardly I am steadily being torn to pieces. Outwardly I read, "They know about you. They'll get you home. It'll be okay." And have no idea what's really happening.

Othman finds various minor ways to abuse me, not bone-breaking ones, but abuses that cause humiliation as well as physical pain sometimes. He leaves me lying on the toilet and doesn't respond to my calls for assistance. Every so often he takes away the chair that supports my left leg, which sticks out of the bed, and lets the leg hang there bent in the air, supported only by my increasingly withered thigh muscles, as the pain quickly intensifies.

But worst of all is not knowing how long I will stay in solitary this time. Will these walls again keep closing in on me for a week or more?

On the afternoon of the third day, with Sayeed not having been to see me even once, guards enter the cell and transfer me back to the big room by the usual method. Othman is waiting for me there.

I ignore him. And then he says to me, "Is there anything you want, Captain?" I admire his ability to swiftly adapt himself to the latest situation.

At nine in the evening, the door to the room opens. Aziz and Sayeed come in. Aziz looks very angry. He places his briefcase on the table, pulls out an issue of *Yediot Ahronot*, flings it in front of me and says, "Read."

An Israeli newspaper? In prison? I haven't seen Hebrew since the prayer book was taken away from me at the hospital. A newspaper? I'm afraid to touch it. They must have found a paper with an article about me from the time of the Six Day War and have seen through my lies. I don't move. I don't breathe.

"Read," Aziz orders me impatiently. I lie there frozen.

"Read," Aziz says again, louder.

I scoot up into a half-sitting position, as much as my plaster cast will allow, and pick up the newspaper. On the back page is an article circled in red. This is the one I am supposed to read. But right above it, at the top of the page, is an article by Eitan Haber—about the two captive pilots in Egypt! My eyes begin to read this article. It is quite lengthy; it says that a Red Cross representative has already met with Nissim Ashkenazi but has not yet met with Giora Romm. It tells of the efforts being made for such a meeting to take place. Whichever intelligence personnel supplied Aziz with this newspaper somehow missed this article in which I am mentioned. I skim the article as fast as I can.

Aziz, seeing where my eyes are directed, scolds me and says I'm not reading the right article, but I just have to finish this unexpected greeting from Israel. When I finish, I start reading the marked article. It is about the arrival of former *Mahal*—foreign volunteer—pilots in Israel for a visit. Men who flew Flying Fortress bombers in the War of Independence as part

of the 69th Squadron and have now come to be the guests of
honor at the inaugural events for the new 69th Squadron—the
IAF's second Phantom squadron. The article also says that this
delegation of elder pilots was hosted at a nostalgic reception by
Prime Minister Golda Meir.

It hits me all at once. The sigh of relief that this isn't about
my past being revealed. The article about me in the Israeli
newspaper. The story about the foreign pilots. What a huge
reprieve! I lie back, look at Aziz and smile. I am certain that he
has brought me this article as a conciliatory gesture.

"Nice story," I say to him. He looks just as angry as before.

"You see," he says to me, "since 1948 you Israelis have
been relying on American pilots. And now they are coming
again. And being welcomed by Mrs. Meir. And you deny that
you are aided by American pilots and you lie to us."

I am quite taken aback. Aziz apparently sees the American
pilots' arrival in Israel as a mirror image of the role played in
Egypt by Russian pilots—i.e., if we here in Egypt are aided by
Soviet pilots, then the Israeli Air Force must be aided in the
same way by American pilots. One must be lightning quick
to grasp and adjust to the ever-changing dimensions of the
situation in the room. Now I see the argument with which I
must contend. But another part of me is still trying to drink
in something more from the newspaper and to feel connected,
if only for a moment, to what is happening in Israel. I think I
catch something about an explosion at a bus stop in Kfar Sava
or something like that. But Aziz yanks the newspaper away
from me.

I lie on my back in the bed. Only a few hours before, I
was still in solitary confinement. My body still reeks from it.
Now I read about myself in an Israeli newspaper. Six weeks I've
been here and I'm still someone else in their eyes. I am holding
my own versus Aziz, whose diligence, attention to detail,

and especially his unyielding resolve to extract from me the maximum possible, I have learned not to underestimate. I want a rest. Aziz interprets my reclining this way as part and parcel of my announcement that I won't talk anymore. I address him as I stare at the ceiling, flooding my brain with the image of the Hebrew letters I read just five minutes before. "Yes, I will answer your questions, Mr. Aziz, but you should know that you have already completely emptied me of anything of value."

They know in Israel that I'm alive, I tell myself at the same time, finally free of that shadow of a doubt that still gnawed at me at times. Life in Israel goes on. I can close my eyes and see the event at Ramat David honoring the 69th Squadron. Did they think to invite Miriam to attend?

Aziz begins to question me about subjects that do not seem too volatile and which allow me to indulge in my favorite pastime—giving long answers filled with utterly trivial details that have nothing really to do with me. I am asked about the Nahal Yam outpost and the tall antennas located there, about the purpose of the naval Gadna's cruise to Cyprus (I give a twenty-minute lecture all about what the Gadna "youth battalions" are and how this program fits into Israeli high school life), about the skydiving training for the paratroopers, and so on.

And then, suddenly, Aziz says to me quietly, "Captain, the airport in Herzliya is used for agricultural aircraft, not for combat planes." For the thousandth time, I die on the spot, but outwardly not a single muscle in my face so much as twitches. I tell him a tale about the two airports in Herzliya, the "white airport" and the "red airport." The "white airport" is the actual civil aviation airport in Herzliya for light aircraft. The "red airport" however, is located about ten kilometers north of the "white" one and is just a remnant of a runway left over from the British Mandate days. In the pilots' course we used to train there for emergency landings, without landing on it of course. From that little strip of reddish-brown earth, the source of the place's nickname, I go about constructing a state-of-the-art military airport in regular use by the air force, as I pray for the evening to end.

Finally Aziz gets up to leave. He reaches the door and opens it, but then turns around and asks me if I know a pilot by the name of Ezra Aharon. Ezra Aharon was Miriam's commander in the air force. He is a Mirage pilot in the 101st Squadron.

"Of course I don't know him, Mr. Aziz, I've never heard that name before."

Aziz goes out and closes the door behind him. *Ezra Aharon? Where did this come from? Is he a POW too? If so, he will surely bring my whole story tumbling down. If he was captured, were all his documents captured too? And if he crashed somewhere in Egypt, God forbid, what did he have in his plane that could incriminate me?* If I thought I would sleep well this night, Aziz's probing about the Herzliya airport and his parting question about Ezra spells the end of that. Now I am wide awake and restless. I send Sami to bring a towel soaked in warm water and he starts to clean me.

The interrogations continue nightly, and Aziz's questions come at me from all directions. I feel the tapestry of my false answers being stretched wider and wider, and I am starting to lose my grip on it. The hundreds of answers I've given that I must remember by heart, combined with the feeling that at any given moment in this dogfight the other side has the "speed and altitude advantage," is increasingly unnerving me. I am completely on edge and dread the impending interrogation every evening. How long will I be caught in this battle for survival? The fact that I'm lying on a normal bed with a mattress doesn't delude me into thinking that my situation is good.

Sometimes, when I'm about to fall apart, and when my guard is not in the room, I push the sheet off and pivot on my back ninety degrees to the left, so that both my legs, which are bolted together, are protruding from the bed. And then, aided by the weight of those plaster casts, I lower myself onto the floor. I stand mainly on my left foot, resting my mid-section against the bed. My head spins but it's worth it just to be upright—as if I mean to escape—and not to lie forever on my back. I can't get myself back in bed so I remain in this position, completely naked, weak and perspiring—until Othman or Sami comes in the room and, in a state of alarm, rushes over to me and lifts me back into bed.

After a few intensive days of questioning, the door does not open at nine the next night for the interrogation to continue. Two days go by, and nothing happens. I'm keeping track of time on the plaster cast over my abdomen. Each day that passes becomes a little notch, and Saturday is the diagonal line that marks off the group of days. I know what day of the week it is. I know the English date. I have no idea what day it is on the Hebrew calendar. I know that I've passed the whole period of the Jewish holidays—for the first time without feeling them at all. Not that I would have considered doing anything special to mark Yom Kippur or Sukkot in here.

Today is Day 45 and the disconnect between whatever Israeli efforts are going on to get me home and what is actually happening to me in Abbasiya Prison is sapping my strength more each day. Sami and Othman treat me appropriately. In time, I learn some words in Arabic to help me communicate with them: *kursi* (chair), *sirir* (mattress), *el quza el tartor* (the can for the pee-pee) and other words for objects that I see in the room. Not much goes on during the day, and most of my time is spent picturing potential scenarios for what will happen from here on. Each one is worse than the previous.

On the night of the forty-eighth day, the outer door of the room opens wide. A minibus is parked there with its rear door opened toward my room. Four soldiers come in with a gurney, blindfold me and transfer me to the floor of the minibus. The doors slam shut, the soldiers sit down on either side of me and the minibus sets off.

Seventeen

29-OCT-1969

I've learned to see through my blindfold, and on the drive west towards Cairo, through the right-side windows of the minibus I saw the ancient Al-Qala' fortress looming over the eastern entry into the city, lit up by spotlights from its base to the top of its turrets. I also saw the darkened buildings of Cairo. They reminded me of the kind of buildings you see in the Florentin neighborhood in Tel Aviv. They seemed to droop with age and weariness, though I realized I ought not to generalize about the whole big metropolis from that one small glimpse. Now, without the offending blindfold, it's much better. My eyes are wide open as I am transferred from the depths of the vehicle to the rolling gurney that awaits me on the asphalt plaza outside. I immediately recognize the main entrance to Al-Maadi Hospital—my hospital. Mine. Here I underwent surgery. Here I made a partial recovery. Here I met Nadia, and Aisha, and Dr. Absalem who never said a word to me, and all the other nurses, and Ali the guard who peeled the orange for me at lunch, and the hospital barber.

I feel like I'm coming home. The gurney is taken inside and I gaze with much curiosity at what is happening in the lobby with the round green pillars. No one gets excited by the sight of my gurney moving toward the elevator fronted by the iron gate. I search for a familiar face but it's obviously a hopeless cause. I have this idea that I'm going to be taken back to the room where I lived for two weeks before being shipped off to prison, as if a large room in an Egyptian hospital would be set aside just for further developments in the biography of Captain Giora Romm.

I am taken to a totally different room, of course. It's a nice room with one bed that is waiting for me, tall drapes along the left wall and two security guards, as usual. One is an older man with a neatly trimmed and groomed mustache. The other is a pleasant-looking younger fellow whom I take to be a college student doing this job for extra income. No one explains to me why I've been brought here, and my guess is that it's for some sort of medical checkup or maybe even to have the cast on my left arm removed.

Two nurses enter the room. Nadia isn't one of them. In fact, I haven't seen either of them before. The understanding starts to sink in that my instinctive desire for continuity, for a feeling of belonging, for some sort of constancy, is not going to be fulfilled. I'm in a different wing, in a different department, with a different staff. The two nurses set up the bowls of water and towels and start to bathe and clean me. In half an hour, I'm as pristine as a newborn, with no trace of the filth and stench that built up under Sami and Othman's watch. One of the nurses serves me the hospital dinner. Eating while lying on clean linens and being clean myself, and in a room that is not a prison cell, instills a feeling of calm. Just the opposite of the feeling of coming totally undone that was my state of being for the past week. When I'm done eating I subject myself to a more comprehensive review.

It's easy to see that I've lost a substantial amount of weight. A good deal of space has opened up between the cast and my hips and stomach. The same thing has happened around my thighs, and it's obvious that my muscles are withering. Moreover, the cotton wool padding between the cast and my body has lost its thickness and I can feel myself shifting about inside a cast that is starting to seem like a separate entity from me. I share these thoughts with the two nurses and they "re-upholster" me by filling all the spaces with cotton wool until they're stuffed nearly to bursting. I feel like I'm being put through a regular maintenance procedure, like the one the Mirage undergoes after every hundred hours of flight, but I have no idea why. No one offers me any information. Night comes and I lay my head back, pleased about the positive change. Right now, nothing else matters to me. I fall asleep.

The next morning gets underway early. Again the nurses—two new ones I don't know, again breakfast and a change of sheets and right after that the hospital barber. This is the barber who shaved me when I was in the hospital the first time, and I note the sense of stability that this return encounter brings. He gets started and then points to my mustache, grimacing to show his lack of admiration. I tell him to shave off the mustache too and he happily complies. As soon as the barber leaves, Sayeed comes in—in his cheerful incarnation this time. He starts to make some general small talk but I cut him off...

"Sayeed, what's this all about?"

"Soon you'll be meeting the Red Cross man. We are scrupulously upholding the agreement we made with you." Then I guess the stint in solitary confinement and all that happened there must have been part of some secret addendum to our agreement. But by now I know which thoughts to speak aloud and which not to, and I keep this one to myself.

Sayeed leaves. Ten minutes later, the door opens and in comes a group of about ten men, all wearing green hospital robes over their clothes. It's easy to pick out the Red Cross fellow. He stands out from the rest with his European attire that's not fully hidden by the green robe, his light complexion and his wavy hair. His name is Monsieur Boisard and he is Swiss like all Red Cross officials, as I learned later. The other men are a mixture of Egyptian intelligence personnel and media people—newspaper reporters, photographers, cameramen and radio technicians with recording equipment.

Boisard introduces himself. I immediately start telling him how happy I am to meet someone from the Red Cross, but he quickly stops me, taking me by surprise, "First I need for you to be convinced that I am really from the Red Cross and not an impostor." He bends down to me and whispers in my ear two words that are private words between Miriam and me.

"That's from your wife," he tells me.

I am very upset with myself for not having even considered the possibility of fraud here. Seven weeks of constant wariness and suspicion, and then all at once I'm ready to walk headlong, unthinking, with open arms and eyes closed, towards the vision of joy that beckons. And my state of mind at this moment cannot be described as anything other than utter joy. Joy in its purest form. I am part of an international system—I may not have any influence over it, but I am still a part of it. I have a line of communication to Israel. To my family. To my friends. To my past.

The hubbub in the room continues as Boisard sits down next to my bed and starts talking with me. He mostly wants to hear about my injuries and about the medical treatment I've received, and he gives me some general information about my family back in Israel. As we converse, we are photographed from every possible angle. Our conversation is interrupted for a moment by a man from Egyptian television who asks me if

I wish to be interviewed for the evening news. I immediately say no, for fear that whatever I say will be edited to make it sound like I am praising my captors. I don't believe I have the strength to go ahead and describe *all* that I've been through, only to have that part be cut out while I am left to languish here after having hurled mud at my hosts and revealed how they pressured me during my time in prison.

The group is asked to leave the room and now it is just Boisard, Sayeed and me. Boisard asks me if we can continue with this ensemble, or whether I would prefer to remain with him alone.

"With you alone, of course," I reply, and Sayeed glares at me and leaves the room too. Boisard pulls out of his briefcase three Red Cross postcards and suggests that I write to my loved ones in Israel. Who shall I write to? Whose name shall I put down? How can I make them understand what's happening to me without really describing it? How can I reassure them— and at the same time ensure they know that I'm not exactly living the good life here? I look up at Boisard and he tells me that the postcards will be examined by the Egyptians. On the postcards is an indication of the maximum number of words allowed—no more than twenty-five words. It's obviously going to take some effort to come up with just the right phrasing, to keep it both succinct and meaningful. I ask for the tray that breakfast is served on and concentrate on writing the postcards. I reassure everyone about my health. There's nothing they can do to help me anyway.

I write about how much I miss them. I tell Miriam not to forget to change the oil in the new Ford Escort we bought a few weeks before I became a POW. I mention my two brothers in the postcard to my parents, not using their real names but the names I gave them during my initial interrogation, on my first day in prison. Uri is still doing reserve duty and Amikam will begin his military service about a year from now. I hand the postcards to Boisard with the expectation that they will make it to Israel.

Boisard comes and stands very close to me. Looking me in the eye, he taps two fingers of one hand against the palm of his other hand. His eyes are asking if they are beating and abusing me. "In many ways," I answer him in a whisper. With hand gestures he tries to warn me that he's worried about eavesdropping. I can't be troubled too much about that right now. Waves of sheer joy keep washing over me. I've just closed a seven-week circle during which I was continuously stretched to the very limit—of life, of survival, of being able to maintain my dignity and uphold my commitment to the state and to the air force—and I managed to withstand every challenge.

I ask Boisard with what frequency we will meet from now on. He thinks it will be once every two weeks. Being a novice at this POW business, my inexperience leads me to accept everything I'm told, the good things at least, as solid fact. *O Sancta Simplicitas.* Boisard goes on to explain that the Red Cross will cover all the expenses for my purchases at the "prison canteen." I can already picture myself sending Othman to fetch me a chocolate bar and an orange soda.

An idea occurs to me. I tell Boisard that Miriam's birthday is next month. I request that the Red Cross in Israel send her a bouquet of flowers on that day together with a short note from me. Boisard promises that it will be done.

The meeting with Boisard lasts for about an hour. He says goodbye and leaves. I expect Sayeed to come back in and say a few words. Sayeed does not return and instead, two security guards enter as usual. To me they are invisible. I am still in the grip of the experience I've just had—trying to take in the fact that up until seven weeks ago, when I joined the worldwide brotherhood of those dependent upon the Red Cross, the very idea of something like this was unreal to me. And now I am overcome with the sense of having achieved a major personal victory, and reveling in feeling connected, even if through a third party, with my loved ones in Israel. I try to find parallels from earlier in my life to what I'm feeling right now. I may still be a POW in Egypt, but I perceive the meeting with the Red Cross as a huge triumph in a horrendously difficult fight. I've faced some tough situations in the past, often emerging from them only by sheer luck, but none of those struggles compares to the profound and utter loneliness with which I've been doing battle for the last forty-nine days, and no other triumph is as sweet as this one. I have no one with whom to share my whirlwind of emotions so I must return to my default state of total self-control. The only people I see are the nurses who bring me my food and the guards who stay with me in the room.

I have no idea if the prison chapter is behind me. What will happen now? Where will I be? My two guards are playing backgammon and I lift my head to try to watch. The one with the neat mustache asks me if I know the game. I say yes and right away he brings the board over to me. He pulls up a small table, arranges the pieces and rolls the dice with a flurry of movements that would put circus jugglers to shame. We start to play.

In the squadron I've certainly never been known for my prowess at backgammon. But what do you know—I win the first game. We start a second game. The younger fellow comes over and sits down behind the shoulder of the mustachioed guard, assuming the pose of a student with his mentor. My opponent shakes the dice with a flourish. Sometimes he blows on them. Sometimes he holds his hand lower than the table top and tosses the dice from below so they land right in the center of the board. Sometimes he waves his hands in circles over his head and then flings the dice on the board. I watch the acrobatics in awe and make a mental note that as soon as I get back to Israel I must describe all these moves to the squadron mechanics at the readiness shelter, where backgammon tournaments are an essential part of the admissions process.

My victory in the second game is by a much larger margin than in the first. Mr. Mustache's demeanor abruptly changes. Now I've gone and done it—I've offended his honor and the honor of Egypt and have clearly gotten myself into more trouble unnecessarily. I needn't turn everything into a contest of nations. I make sure to lose the next four games, and I need all four losses, because only after the fourth loss is the friendly mood finally restored. Mr. Mustache is able to withdraw to the guards' corner as the clear victor, and the younger guard stays to talk with me. He is in fact a student at Al-Azhar University. He is studying psychology. He doesn't know Israel, but he of course knows about the map in the Knesset showing Israel stretching from the Nile to the Euphrates. Suddenly I feel like one of those traveling speakers from the Jewish Agency who go from one American Jewish community to another telling the same stories, hearing the same questions and giving the same answers. On this day, however, I don't have the patience to play that role, and our conversation is grounded shortly after takeoff.

They turn out the light in the room and still I have trouble falling asleep. I keep replaying the meeting with Boisard in my mind again and again. I start to think that I didn't extract the maximum information that I could have from him. I didn't manage the meeting as well as I could have. Maybe I didn't ask everything I could have asked. Maybe I didn't convey through him all that I could have conveyed. But that's water under the bridge now. I lie here in the darkness until sleep finally overtakes me.

Early the next day, the nurses push aside the drapes and I behold a balcony and beyond that the sprawling city of Cairo, shrouded in morning mist. Again they bathe me and serve me the hospital breakfast. I brace myself for another day here, as

I think about how I might further improve my situation and what I ought to ask for. The door opens and Sayeed comes in. He wants me to know that I deeply offended him yesterday when I wouldn't let him stay in the room during the meeting with Boisard. I tell him that if he ever has a meeting with a Red Cross representative in Israel, after seven weeks of waiting, I promise to leave the room.

He looks at me for a few seconds and breaks into a wide grin. I know that he, more than others, has come to be fond of me, and I allow myself to say things around him that I wouldn't say to anyone else.

While Sayeed is still in the room, Dr. Absalem comes in. It struck me before that his name is the Arabic version of Absalom. And each time I see him the thought that he bears an almost identical name to that of King David's son gives me the chills. I can't help contrasting his bald head with Absalom's flowing locks, and I'm pretty certain that this isn't the only way the two diverge.

Absalem has come by for a standard doctor's visit. This time I don't let him go so easily and I force him to talk to me. I request an explanation of the injuries to my leg and elbow. Absalem gives me a very optimistic prognosis. As for my hand, he says that the cast can come off fifty-five days after the surgery. Throughout the conversation he keeps his distance from me and avoids making even the slightest friendly gesture. Perhaps we killed his brother with a shot to the back too, like Sami's brother. Who knows?

As evening comes, just when it gets dark, it all comes crashing down. Four soldiers come to take me away, and I know that I'm headed back to prison, to my true home.

Eighteen

31-OCT-1969

I lie in the big room in the prison, still replaying the last two days in the hospital and the meeting with Monsieur Boisard. For a fleeting moment, I'd been plucked from the lowest depths and had a measure of my dignity restored. More than anything, it was the private meeting with Boisard, after I sent Sayeed out of the room, that transformed the worthless speck that had lain there so completely alone in solitary confinement back into a whole human being. I understand that prison is to be my permanent home but I know that it has many faces and I cherish the hope that from this point on I will stay in the big room, free of harassment, until I am returned to Israel.

Sami gets things set up in the room and then he brings me dinner. He is still quite upset that I have come back sans mustache and says that Othman will take it hard. Then he asks me to tell him what happened to me while I was away.

While we're talking, the door opens. Sayeed is standing there and behind him is another jailer carrying a cardboard box. They come over to my bed and begin unpacking the box and arranging the contents on the bedside table. These are the things that Miriam sent me from Israel or, to be more precise, some of the things that Miriam sent me from Israel.

First Sayeed takes out some unremarkable items, mostly articles of clothing like rubber flip-flops, underwear and trousers. Then he takes out packages of candy and a carton of Kent cigarettes. But then comes the crowning glory: two books—a Hebrew copy of *A Simple Story* by the Israeli author S. Y. Agnon who was the Nobel Prize laureate three years prior and *Winnie the Pooh* in English. This is overwhelming. Seeing the Agnon book instantly makes me lose all desire to talk to anyone or do anything else but lose myself in it. I exchange a few polite words with Sayeed and as soon as he leaves the room I open it to the first page and start reading. By three in the morning I've finished the whole book. I've accompanied Hirschl through all his trials and tribulations, amid the air of tragedy that permeates the work from start to finish. But rather than analyze Hirschl's character that much, I've simply been under the spell of that connection that happens between book and reader. I know that I will reread it many times, and that with each reading, I will discover new dimensions and layers of meaning. But right now, it is more than just a book; it is another link to the world I came from, to the world I grew up in, and it is the antithesis of the back page of *Al Jumhuriya*, the newspaper that Othman "reads" every morning at the desk in front of my bed, with the anti-Israeli cartoon that he always relishes sharing with me.

I wake up the next morning as the owner of personal property in this prison. I glance to my right—everything is still there on the bedside table, including the carton of cigarettes that was sent to a non-smoker POW. Sayeed surprises me with another visit. He asks if I remember my promise—that after the meeting with the Red Cross I would tell them things I know even if not specifically asked about them. I tell Sayeed that the most efficient way to do this would be to give me a paper and pencil, and whenever I remember something, I will write it down. In five minutes, paper and pencil appear on the bedside table. When Sayeed leaves, I start jotting down random numbers and letters, in a kind of ritual reclaiming of my writing ability.

On one sheet of paper I sketch a chess board. I vaguely recall Stefan Zweig's story *The Chess Story* about a prisoner held in total isolation for many months who maintains his sanity by playing imaginary games of chess. I can't see, though, how I could play a game of chess against myself, not to mention how I could fashion the pieces, and especially, how I could do all this without attracting Othman's attention. I decide to convert the chess idea into checkers. The game pieces are easier to make. Every morning I take tiny leftover bits of pita and flatten them with my fingers to create the white pieces. For the black ones I have another solution. I take the remaining drops of jam from breakfast and smear them on the plaster cast over my stomach. No fly in the room can withstand the temptation, and using one of the rubber flip-flops I kill eight flies each morning so I have eight new black pieces for the day. I keep the paper game board folded inside the cast on my left arm, and only when Othman or Sami has left the room do I extract it from its hiding place. I make a little tent by putting a pillow on either side of me to prop up the sheet that covers me, then I unfold and smooth out the board atop the cast on my stomach, arrange the white pita pieces and the black crushed-fly pieces, and focus on developing some interesting moves in a game of checkers.

On the second evening, I start reading *Winnie the Pooh*, a book I somehow missed when I was a child. At first I'm a little annoyed by the childishness of this material that I've been given and presume it to be a devious Egyptian selection meant just to rile me. But as I get further along in the book, I become attached to Pooh and his friends in a way that's hard to describe. The wisdom that jumps off each page delights me no end. But instead of just deriving pleasure from the book, I can't help but feel angry with myself for not having read it when I was younger. Pooh and his friends give me optimism and faith that in the end, there is something good and pure in everyone.

I take up smoking.

Many days ago, before the meeting with the Red Cross, my guards noticed that I was always asking what time it was. They began setting their watches back or ahead, or wearing them on the inside of their wrists, and they often bring me my meals at odd hours—all to make me lose the sense of time. I decide to use the cigarettes as a substitute for a watch. I tell Sami and Othman that I'm going to start smoking, but to avoid becoming hooked I will only smoke one cigarette every four hours. They shall be responsible for strictly keeping track of my smoking time.

I have time to eat some of the candy I received and to read and reread both books. Nothing more is happening with the interrogations and I'm relieved that they seem to be behind me. Each day I am filled with a keen hope that the following day will bring another meeting with the Red Cross. The days and nights pass with long talks with each of my guards, who gradually tell me more about their private lives. Sami is again the one who is more eager to talk about personal things. This time it's about what a heavy smoker he is, and we spend a long time discussing how he can cut down. Eventually I order him, as an officer, to smoke one cigarette with me every four hours, plus I give him permission to smoke one more cigarette after two hours. Othman insists on telling me about the movies he's seen. He plants himself right in front of me, speaks in a mixture of Arabic and fragmented English and fills in the rest with exaggerated physical demonstrations. What I wouldn't give to bring Othman to entertain at our annual air force staff party.

After a week Sayeed comes back and brings me another package. This one, too, has two books—*The House at Pooh Corner*, the sequel to *Winnie the Pooh*, and Ibsen's play *Peer Gynt*, in English, that have been selected for me, as I shall learn later upon my return to Israel, by my friend Ilan Kutz. I also ask for and am given back the prayer book and I begin reciting daily all the prayers that are incumbent upon a pious Jew, from the morning blessings to the bedtime *shema*. In time I find that I know by heart the *shemona-esrei* and the Grace after Meals, which I say every time after eating, even if not required by Jewish law. But while the days pass seemingly without any immediate threat, I can't stop thinking about the meeting with the Red Cross that isn't happening, and about Sayeed, who has ceased making any appearances.

All I can do is to try to occupy myself with constructing a picture of the world from the sounds around me—the songs of Umm Kulthum over the prison loudspeakers, the distant noise of the train, the rumbling of what I take to be the supply truck that arrives each morning and maneuvers into position in the lot on the other side of the wall, the call of the muezzin five times a day, and so on. My favorite thing to listen to is the guards' physical fitness training. All I hear is the trainer calling out, "*Wahad, tnein, tlata*" —one, two, three—and then everyone calling out in unison, "Wahad." Then the trainer counts again and everyone answers, "Tnein." And he calls out once more and this time the chorus of soldiers finishes off the count with, "Tlata." I can just picture all the Samis and Othmans doing exactly the same exercises that we do in our fitness training. Othman comes directly to my room after the session, collapses onto his chair sweating and faces me with his slightly menacing smile. As if somehow sensing that I, in my state of total incapacitation, am mocking his exposure as a lowly soldier who was just put through the most basic exercise drills, like obedient soldiers the world over.

One day, in the afternoon, Othman is fiddling with the dial of the radio in the guards' lounge adjacent to my room. He pauses for a few seconds at each clear frequency and then proceeds to search for the next one. And then, when he stops at one frequency, I hear the announcer saying loud and clear, in Hebrew: "…And from the Kiryat Haim stadium we now take you back to the studio in Jerusalem…" before he turns the dial again. The jolt hits me with the force of the missile that struck my plane. Few things have made the reality of captivity hit home more acutely than this tiny fleeting episode. It suddenly strikes me that my country is really divided into two camps: one is made up of all the other citizens who are going about their normal daily life, and then there's me—lying here in such total and miserable isolation. Back in Israel soccer games are still being played, people are going out shopping, friends are getting together, on Fridays there are parties, and no one there has the least clue about me and what I'm going through.

Depression overtakes me, and it deepens by the hour. I can't shake off those words that I heard, I can't shake off the knowledge that just twenty feet from my bed is a dial that I could turn to get to hear Israel Radio. I can't shake off the thing that frightens me the most—that my captivity has a known starting date but no clear end date whatsoever. This is the sword of Damocles that hangs over the head of every POW.

The days go by and my disappointment at Boisard's

failure to reappear gives way to an understanding that this whole thing is far from over. The awareness gradually sinks in that Boisard's absence is due to something more than a simple scheduling problem. Something deeper than that is going on, and I don't have the slightest idea what it could be. And heightening my distress, as usual, is the fact that I have no friend or acquaintance with whom to consult, no one to talk to and share my thoughts with. The loneliness, even when Sami or Othman is with me, steadily gnaws away at me. I begin to feel embarrassed by my eager anticipation that any day might be the day I meet Boisard. It starts to build each morning when every little rustling near the room's main door makes me all alert and tense in my bed, and my heart flutters with the hope that perhaps he is coming now. And when night approaches, and with it the time for the bedtime prayers, I can feel that crushing blend of disappointment and fear slithering at me from every corner, and I have nowhere to hide.

Nineteen

9-NOV-1969

The door opens and there stands Aziz. Aziz thinks that since there has been no progress in my case, we might as well use the time to resume our talks.

I am in shock. The prospect of being subjected to a new round of interrogation has terrified me day in and day out. I've envisioned networks of Egyptian spies in Israel under orders to find the exact location of the Herzliya Air Base. I've imagined an Egyptian building contractor sauntering into the room to discuss our mutual profession, a profession I know nothing about. I've pictured phone calls placed from Egyptian embassies in Europe to phone numbers in Israel gleaned from my earlier interrogations, none of them leading to the intended recipient. And now Aziz is standing here in front of me, not late at night as I have always seen him before, but in the middle of the afternoon, casually suggesting that we resume the process, a process in which I might cause serious harm to the Israeli Air Force. I answer him tersely that I am not ready to talk. I tell him that we made an agreement and we kept it. An easy yes from me to his prodding now will only be perceived as an admission that I really do have much more to say. And I don't. Didn't I already convincingly tell them that I've divulged everything I know? He tells me I'm making a mistake and leaves the room. I understand the code.

I'm going back to solitary confinement.

But no—nothing more happens until the evening. In the evening, Sayeed stops by along with another man I don't recognize. Sayeed makes some small talk and then asks to hear an account of what happened when I ejected from my stricken plane. He professes astonishment that I broke my leg.

"I wouldn't expect someone like you to break his leg."

His remarks are odd and disconnected from reality. When I explain that my thigh was shattered during the ejection process, the two of them express great surprise that I was able to make a parachute landing on just one leg. But then they hasten to add that it's not really all that surprising. For who, if not I, could manage to land smoothly on one leg without breaking the other one? If I had a mirror I would take a good look at my reflected image to make sure that it is I with whom they are having this bizarre conversation. What did I do to deserve all this praise? And what the hell is the purpose of this conversation? Sayeed says that the more they come to know me, the more they admire me, especially my outstanding parachuting abilities. In my very first interrogation, I said that I had never parachuted before.

The next afternoon, the door opens and Aziz and Sayeed enter with very stern expressions. Aziz pulls a thick stack of papers out of his leather briefcase and whacks it down on the desk.

"You lied to us nonstop!" he shouts. He picks up the pile, waves it in front of me and angrily hurls it on the floor, causing the pages to scatter. "These are the pages of your answers and they are a collection of lies!"

My heart pounds wildly. Not only is there no chance now of a second meeting with the Red Cross, but something unknown has happened, something that has dramatically changed my situation. I can't manage to utter a sound. Aziz is a seething mass of red-hot fury and keeps demanding that I start telling the truth. I muster up enough courage to say that I have never lied, and as I do so Aziz grabs his briefcase and leaves the room with Sayeed, leaving the papers strewn all over the floor.

I know it won't be long now until I am hauled back to solitary, and I come up with a stupid idea. To counter the loneliness and boredom of solitary confinement, I slide the copy of *The House at Pooh Corner* inside my cast, under the part that covers my abdomen. I picture myself lying there in solitary reading a book to help pass the endless lonely hours. Screwing the system. Just after I've slipped the book inside, the usual assemblage of guards enters the room, and in minutes I am back on the concrete bed in solitary.

Othman, who'd lately been receiving some of the candies from my bedside on a regular basis and consequently became a bit less rough and a bit more pleasant, is particularly nasty to me. He knows all my physical limitations and decides to put me through a series of minor abuses in the time he has left before Sami comes to relieve him. My guess is that these are the orders he received from his superiors. But I still retain some naïve thinking about values and friendship and am surprised once again at how the friendship we built up over the past weeks is shot to pieces the moment I'm tossed back into solitary.

Sami comes in the evening. He spares me the harassment, but he isn't about to sit with me or speak with me. When I hear his footsteps receding, I pull the book out of the space between my abdomen and the cast and start to read. Before a minute has gone by, I know there's no way I'll be able to keep on. The thought that someone could quietly slide open the panel in the door, look in on me and see what I'm up to utterly terrifies me. I quickly bury the book inside the cotton wool over my stomach. I search for a way to get rid of it but there is no solution that I can see. I'm doomed to lie here with this hot potato on my stomach until either I'm brought back to the big room or its existence is discovered. And then god only knows what will be done to me.

Meanwhile, I still have no way of knowing just what has changed. All I know is that I'm back to the dreaded routine of being trapped inside two dungeons at once, my plaster prison and solitary confinement.

It's the start of the Muslim holy month of Ramadan and this changes the tune of the muezzin's calls. His warbling during these fast days is more musically pleasant, and as he chants his final call of the day my thoughts drift to Boisard, to my books, to the candies and cigarettes that were left on the little bedside table… and I fall asleep.

Twenty

10-NOV-1969

The next morning passes in total quiet. Back to the routine of *aysh we-gebna* with a mug of water, back to just lying there listening to Koranic verses and the calls of the muezzin. Back to *The House at Pooh Corner* still stuck inside my cast—I can't stop cursing my arrogance in thinking I could outsmart my captors this way. As if I would ever be able to proudly boast of this little exploit to anyone in Egypt. Being about the only thing to focus on in the silence of the cell, it takes on the usual characteristics of a "problem"— inexorably growing in magnitude until it induces panic.

Will I be able to get through the whole time here without the book being discovered? And if it is discovered, what else could be done to me? Is there another dungeon worse than this one to which they take prisoners who've earned further sanctions? Or will they just extend my stay here two or three times longer than planned? At this point, the book ceases to be the main problem. Now the main problem is how to get a grip on my anxiety, including its physical symptoms—the accelerated breathing, the perspiration, the darting glances all around the cell in the vain hope of finding some secret cranny in which to toss this unwanted baggage.

In the afternoon the door opens and Aziz enters. He chooses not to come all the way across the cell and stand in front of me. Instead he stands directly behind my head so that I must regard him completely from below. He is dressed for winter, quite fancily in a heavyweight checked jacket and a tie, and jutting from his mouth is a thin Tiparillo cigar, the kind that comes with a white plastic mouthpiece. I like to smoke these thin cigars and I'm certain that Miriam sent them for me. He stands there staring at me, underscoring the vast disparity between his status and mine. As if I needed any further illustration of this.

We have a brief conversation in which I repeat my demand to see the Red Cross. Outwardly this demand is presented forcefully, but inside I feel like my body is steadily turning to mush, that it is losing its solidity due to the cruel ravages of my situation and the steep slope down which I've tumbled—from the hospital room back to the big room in the prison and now back here, to my solitary dungeon. Aziz exhales one more puff of smoke and quietly exits the cell. The hours pass and no one else comes in. I dine on another round of ant-speckled pita with salty cheese, the day nears its end and I begin to contemplate sleep.

But then the door opens and in walks a giant I've never seen in the prison before. He is very dark-skinned. I surmise that he is of Sudanese extraction and is some kind of mid-level prison employee, perhaps yet another person who just wants to get a peek at the Zionist captive. But no. He stands over me and begins to talk, in a threatening tone and at a decibel level far beyond anything I've experienced here up to now.

"Why don't you want to talk? Who are you not to answer us when we ask you questions?" By now I know enough Arabic to understand what he is saying, though I don't get what this fellow has to do with me. Who the hell is he? Why is he interfering in matters that are between me and Aziz, or at best, between me and Sayeed?

I will talk with Mr. Aziz, I tell him. He keeps shouting at me, speaking faster and faster, getting louder and louder, so that I'm sure they can hear him all over the building, and I'm having trouble understanding him now. Keeping up his relentless stream of words, he leans in closer to me. His physical proximity is making me uneasy and I interrupt him...

"Please, please (a-bliz, a-bliz), I will talk to Mr. Aziz." But he goes right on yammering, his voice continuing to rise. Then out of nowhere he gives my left cheek a powerful openhanded smack, for which I am wholly unprepared. I am shocked into silence. The blow was awful. Utterly frozen, I gape at his hands. They are about the size of ping-pong paddles. He keeps on shouting and then again he raises his hand, aiming the back of it at my right cheek. My right arm, the only limb I can move, springs up to protect my cheek.

"Khudh yidak," says the Sudanese giant. I understand that he is instructing me to take my arm out of the way, before he is forced to move it himself. I put down my right hand and grasp my left hand with it, and the blow immediately follows, this time from the back of his massive hand. My heads whips to the left and my cheek burns. The Sudanese goes on talking. Whatever he is saying sounds increasingly aggressive. He readies his hand to strike my left cheek. My right hand flies up to protect my face.

"*Khudh yidak,*" he repeats the order from before. Again I clutch my left hand and the blow arrives. I gaze at him in disbelief—*Who are you to suddenly come in here and beat me? What is going on here?* He continues striking me as I look straight into his eyes. Not because I'm such a big hero but because I'm flat on my back and he is bending over me, with a menacing expression, staring me right in the face. The humiliation of it kicks me hard in the gut. Here I lie in a dungeon in Egypt, and this huge Sudanese fellow whom I wouldn't give a second glance to in normal life is hard at work destroying my face. He never stops jabbering for a moment as he gets into a rhythm of hitting me, each blow harder than the one before, alternating between one cheek and the other, with another cuff coming about every thirty seconds.

I shift my gaze to the ceiling and start telling myself after each blow *I'm still alive, I'm still alive, I'm still alive.* My head feels like it's coming apart, the sensation just the opposite of the way the bones in an infant's skull gradually fuse. The blows keep landing, right and left, and though I keep telling myself that I'm still alive, I'm wondering if this could be causing me irreversible damage.

My hands are tucked inside the cast over my stomach, holding on tight to *The House at Pooh Corner* and not flying up instinctively to protect my face. If he wants to beat me, let him beat me. I will not make any defensive move.

And the blows just keep on coming and coming.

By my estimation, it goes on for more than twenty minutes. At last, the Sudanese giant straightens up, his forehead and cheeks glistening with sweat. But most frightening of all is the intensity of the hatred with which he glares at me. No one has looked at me this way since I arrived in Egypt, not even Othman during his occasional angry outbursts. He is literally foaming at the mouth, and he slides his finger across his throat.

Nihna nitbihak.

I don't need to be much of an expert in Arabic to catch the meaning of these words. *We will slaughter you.* He repeats them over and over; the finger across the throat gesture becomes more forceful and demonstrative each time. When will it ever end? Finally, he shakes his finger at me, barks, "Talk!," stomps out of the cell and shuts the door behind him.

My head is a wreck and hurting like hell. I feel a peculiar mixture of indignation and satisfaction. Indignation that this Sudanese fellow could just show up all of a sudden and beat me while I am completely defenseless. Satisfaction at the thought that it's been five minutes now since he left, and here is one more thing I have endured and survived in my life in captivity. *I am alive.* Physically, I think I'm okay. My body temperature is broiling, though. The blood is coursing wildly through my veins. I pat my skull and nothing appears to be broken. It just hurts. I lie in the cell in silence. The pain from my throbbing head, the shock of this affront, the hot feeling all through by body, *The House at Pooh Corner* stuck inside my cast, the realization that something has gone seriously wrong—all of it swirls together, keeping me awake for many more hours. I hear the panel in the door above me open quietly and I imagine that Sami wants to see how I'm doing. Usually I turn my head to the left and back to see the eyes peering through the little window, but this time I just lie still. To a certain extent I feel ashamed that I was beaten. I'm still trying to process what just happened and pondering the fact that even though I've already met with the Red Cross, the Egyptians' treatment of me is going from bad to worse.

The next day is seemingly ordinary. Uneventful.

Anyone who's ever been in solitary knows what such days are like. You get your food, you empty your bowels and you lie in total isolation. At around two in the afternoon I start to wonder what the evening will be like. Will the Sudanese giant be back to visit? As the time creeps by, my uneasiness grows.

At some point, the uneasiness morphs into terror. I think if they just told me straight out that another round of beatings would take place "tomorrow at nine," I'd be less afraid than I am in this diabolical situation in which they hold all the cards. In the evening, the Sudanese comes in. There are two differences between this evening and yesterday evening. After I tell him that I am willing to speak with Aziz only, he starts hitting me, but this time he forgoes the incessant shouting. Every so often he blurts something in Arabic, but he's really concentrating on the beating, his expression a mixture of hatred and pleasure.

The other difference is that this time the cell door remains open during the beating. When my head swings around to the left after a particularly sharp blow, to my surprise I spy the prison doctor watching from the other side of the doorway. Our eyes meet for a moment and he steps back. Now I have something new to focus on while the Sudanese giant goes about trying to break my skull. This is all planned. This is all under supervision. This Sudanese fellow, who may at times be excelling at his assignment a bit more than required, was sent by Aziz. But Aziz also sent the prison doctor to ensure that the blows don't cause me excessive harm. It occurs to me that because of the late hour of these beatings, the doctor didn't go home at the end of the workday. The thought also crosses my mind that he may have purposely arranged to have the evening shift tonight just to spice up an otherwise dull stint on duty. I occupy myself with such trivialities in order to defer the real, serious thoughts to a later hour.

The Sudanese guy keeps on pummeling me in the head and I feel my body heating up and know that tonight it will remain warmer than usual. Because of the chilliness of the cell on these November nights, against which the lone sheet that covers me is practically useless, I try to see this as a silver lining. The beating will help me retain my body heat. But when the Sudanese finally finishes and leaves, the awareness immediately hits that I am in some deep shit here. Just what this shit is, I do not know.

The next day the fear starts to build at noon. Will the same formula be repeated? Does the prison's daily schedule again include "9:00 p.m. – A Beating for the Zionist Captain"? I glance at the wall to my right, see the "They know about you..." and start to weave a fantasy that at this very moment two helicopters are secretly making their way to Cairo to rescue me.

Before long this general idea turns highly specific, and features two key details: One—the soldiers will be from the paratroops, and two, when the door opens, Raful[1] himself will be standing there. No one else. It must be Raful. I plan out exactly what I will say to them when they kick the door open; the instructions I will give them on how to transport me in the cast; how I will explain that I must have my healthy right arm around the neck of one of the paratroopers carrying me so that I won't fall. In short—I become completely engrossed in envisioning my rescue operation. I lay my head back, close my eyes and a great feeling of calm comes over me. It almost makes me smile to myself. But around seven in the evening, everything abruptly changes.

---

[1] Lieutenant General Rafael (Raful) Eitan, a legendary paratrooper and warrior who later became chief of staff of the IDF

Twenty-One

13-NOV-1969

I hear dogs barking outside my cell wall. Not a lone dog that's gone astray. Not two dogs engaged in a nocturnal conversation. Not several dogs scattered around various locations in the prison. A large pack of dogs is standing there, right outside my cell wall, and barking like crazy. I know with utter certainty that these dogs were brought to the prison especially for me, and not merely to hinder the paratroopers.

Tonight at nine they won't beat me. Maybe Mrs. Sudanese Giant implored her husband to come home on time tonight and help put the little Sudanese giants to bed. Maybe he was invited over by friends to break the Ramadan fast. Tonight they won't beat me.

Instead they plan to take me out of the cell, lay me down in the center of the yard in the cold, in the gusting wind, on the sand, naked inside my plaster shell, and let the snarling dogs scamper around and have at me at will. I can picture the scene in my mind and with each passing moment it becomes increasingly real. I'm annoyed that the sand will get inside the cast and the cotton wool and afterwards it will be impossible to get it out. I'm terrified of the dogs, which I expect are not quite as disciplined as my Sudanese tormentor. No doctor looking on will be able to react in time if one of the dogs figures out that I'm a Zionist and doesn't stick to the rules. The wind is whistling outside, and thought of lying there in the middle of the sandy yard on such a cold night, completely naked except for the cast, with the pack of dogs surrounding me and moving in closer and closer, is making me fall to pieces.

I can't touch the pita and cheese that Sami brought into the cell. I can feel my heart thudding wildly. I don't know the exact time, but I know that the night activity usually gets going around nine. The dogs keep on barking and running about and I know that tonight my captors are taking off the gloves even more. Time goes by and nothing else happens, however. I wait for ten o'clock to come, and then eleven. Koranic verses blare on the loudspeakers, the rats skitter back and forth above me inside the asbestos ceiling, the dogs keep barking… and at long last I fall asleep, a complete wreck from the mental terror I put myself through for the past five or six hours.

I wake up in the morning somewhat astounded by the realization of what we can do to ourselves. The dogs are gone now but I still can't bring myself to eat breakfast. Othman hands me the can for me to piss into, and stands waiting right next to me as if I'm invisible. He scares me from time to time, this Othman. I've started to hope that the prison doctor will be standing just outside the door when Othman, this unpredictable ticking bomb, really goes off one day. The black crust covers my body again, because of the massive amounts of perspiration I've secreted since my arrival back in solitary, and it's starting to smell.

I've decided that if they beat me tonight I will attempt to fake passing out. I will try to halt the beating by pretending to lose consciousness. But acting is certainly not my forte. How can I pull it off? I figure that letting my eyes close and my body go slack should get the message across.

I remember what Yankele Nahmias, the commander of Israel military intelligence's POW interrogation unit, once told me about a simple way to test whether someone has really fainted or not: You lift the person's head up by the hair and then let go. The head of someone who has truly passed out will drop like a stone. The head of someone who's faking it will brake slightly as it drops since the neck muscles will instinctively tighten in order to soften the fall.

I start to test what it feels like when your head drops like a stone. It's not all that terrible. I lift my head again and let it fall and strike the concrete surface on which I lie. I figure that with enough practice I'll be able to let my head drop like someone who is genuinely unconscious. Again and again I let my head fall back and hit the concrete. The hair on the back of my skull becomes flattened like a sheet of lead. My head is pounding but I must take some initiative and create some kind of change if the Sudanese returns tonight to beat me some more. I hope that the Egyptians use Nahmias' system for testing unconsciousness and not some other method, but I can't be sure. The day creeps by slowly. The message I scratched into the right wall with the dry pita during my last stay here—*They know about you. They'll get you home. It'll be okay.* —is still visible, but I'm no longer so sure that it will be okay.

Towards evening the door behind my head opens. I assume that the Sudanese has returned. But it's Sayeed. He's holding a brown envelope and his expression is serious. He asks how I am. I tell him I'm fine. I ask if he knows what happened in this cell in the last few days. He says not exactly, adding that when a person lies nonstop, he ought not to be surprised if the hospitality he received and enjoyed changes because of the insult to his hosts. I ask him why he thinks I'm lying. He pulls a sheet of paper out of the envelope.

"There is an article in your newspaper that tells who you are. Why did you lie to us?"

Twenty-Two

14-NOV-1969

I ask to see the article. He hands me the sheet of paper. It's the size of a page from a weekend supplement. The page is covered with Arabic writing and taped in the center is a picture that was cut out of a newspaper, showing a skydiver standing in the doorway of a Nord plane—the French transport aircraft used by the Israeli Air Force—in flight. His face is covered by a mask and he wears the soft helmet used by free divers, and he is preparing to leap out of the plane. I stare at it in disbelief.

"What does this have to do with me?"

"It's you," Sayeed says to me. "It's you when you were the Israeli national free diving champion."

It suddenly hits me that this is an article about my friend Giora Epstein, formerly the Israeli national free diving champion and now a Mirage pilot in the 101st Squadron and my neighbor in the family housing quarters at Hatzor Airbase.

"That's not me," I repeat fervently. What a relief! If this is what they have to refute my story then maybe there is a light at the end of this dungeon, though there is still a long way to go until I reach it.

"The article is called 'Giora, King of the Sky,'" Sayeed tells me. "All the details match things you told us about yourself. But why didn't you tell us the whole story? Why did you hide things from us?"

The questions and comments from the past week regarding my parachuting talents suddenly make sense. But how can I get out of this? I ask Sayeed to let me read the article in Hebrew. "Let me read it," I tell him, "and I'll show you right away that it's not me."

"It's you," he says, and then he leaves the cell.

My emotions are all in a whirl. Disgust over the stay in solitary. Anger that an article like this could be published in Israel, with my first name in the main headline, while I am imprisoned here. Fear at what the future holds. Fury that no one in the world seems to care that I'm not getting to meet with the Red Cross. Irritation at constantly hearing Arabic spoken all around me and Koranic verses blaring over the loudspeakers and having my nostrils filled with that cloyingly sweet smell that typifies the Egypt that I know. The plaster cast is becoming increasingly stifling, and all I want is to be around Hebrew speakers who will keep me company when I am so thoroughly grounded.

I remember what Dr. Absalem said about the cast on my left arm needing to remain for fifty-five days. I start peeling it off. This is no small task, but it's something to keep me busy. Of course, I don't have any sharp implement to use, and the challenge is how to make the initial tear in the upper part of it. I scrape at the plaster with my fingernails and discover that the cast is made up of layer upon layer of a mesh-like bandage.

I eventually manage to peel away a good part of the plaster above my elbow only to be greeted by a shocking sight—an emaciated arm with peeling skin and wasted muscles.

I stare at my arm for a long time, proud of what I've accomplished and frightened by how it looks. Sami comes in and has a fit when he sees what I've done. He's all upset and orders me to stop immediately or else he'll tie my hands. I tell him to calm down and he tells me to go to sleep.

"I can't fall asleep with the light on," I tell him. "Turn the light off for me."

Sami has pity on me because of the last few days. "I'm not supposed to do this, but I will turn the light out for you for twenty minutes. You'll fall asleep and then I'll turn it back on and you won't notice."

Sami leaves and turns out the light. For the first time in a week, something in my living conditions has changed for the better. It's dark at night! I have twenty minutes to try to fall asleep. My leaden head lies against the concrete. I close my eyes and tell myself that now there must be only nineteen minutes left, or maybe only eighteen. I regulate my breathing, lightly stroke the exposed part of my left arm and continue with my attempts to fall asleep. Now there's less than fifteen minutes left. The minutes go by and it's hard for me to relax my body in order to sleep. And what happens if I fall asleep and then I wake up as soon as the light is switched back on? My head turns from side to side. Ten more minutes to go. I lie in this restless torment until the entire twenty minutes have passed and the light bulb is finally turned on, putting me out of my agony. Now I close my eyes as usual and fall asleep very quickly.

The next afternoon, Sayeed comes in. I'm uncomfortable receiving visitors in my current residence because I know that my body has a very bad smell. The combination of the black crust that coats my skin, the sores on my scalp, my partially exposed left arm which reeks from the odor of the wrecked plaster—it all puts me into a lowlier position than ever. Othman brings in a chair for Sayeed, and Sayeed sits down and pulls a page from a Hebrew newspaper out of an envelope. He hands it to me and says,

"Read about yourself."

It's a page from *Ha'olam Hazeh* with that infuriating headline "Giora, King of the Sky." In the center of the page is a picture of Giora Epstein. His face is not shown, of course, and cannot be identified. I read the article. Surprisingly, there is quite a bit of overlap between this Giora's exploits and what I've told the Egyptians about myself, including being hit and landing at the Ramat David base during the Six Day War. But this Giora has also downed two planes and done a number of other things that I haven't appropriated for my biography. There's no point in trying to deny those things that can't be denied, but I see that there is one little detail that can prove my case. Giora Epstein and his wife Sara have a young daughter. Miriam and I don't have any children.

I finish reading, wondering just who the Israeli genius was who came up with the idea for this article while I'm a POW here in Egypt, and I say, "It's not me, Sayeed."

"It is you, Captain. It is you."

"And the little girl?" I ask. "Why did I hide her until now?"

"You're a very clever man," Sayeed replies. "But your wife writes about your daughter in every letter."

"Nice try, Sayeed," I say. "My wife doesn't write about any daughter. I'm not as clever as you think, but I'm also not dumb enough to let you tell me fairy tales. My wife doesn't write about any daughter. It's not me. It's another pilot with the same name. When I get back to Israel I'll look him up and I'll make sure to tell him how much you all admire him."

"You must know him if it's not you."

"I don't know him, I don't have a daughter, I'm not a free diver, and you've made a big mistake."

"Captain, even if it's not you, we have a lot of information about what we discussed in the interrogations. You lied to us the whole time."

I make a dismissive gesture and Sayeed moves on to the topic of my cast. I tell him about Dr. Absalem's fifty-five days, and he wants to know where I'm hurrying to.

"You think you're going back to flying?" he asks.

"Absolutely," I tell him. "I'll recover, I'll get back to the shape I was in before I was injured and you'll see me fly." With the firmness of my answers, I try to pull myself out of the downward spiral of the past week and to tell them, and myself to some extent, that this is how an officer of the Israeli Air Force behaves.

Sayeed gets up, pats me on the shoulder and says: "You're clever, you're a liar and I hope you get well."

Twenty-Three

14-NOV-1969

That night, at ten, Sayeed comes in again, this time with Aziz. Two chairs are brought into the cell, and Aziz says to me, "There is no military airport in Herzliya. It's an airfield for agricultural planes. We're going to start the questioning here now, and you will stay in this place until you tell us the truth. What air base are you from?"

He takes a small yellow card out of his briefcase and hands it to me to look at. It's the maintenance card from my ejection seat, it must have been attached to it. The card says: Usable, Air Force Base Number 8. Or, in other words—This ejection seat has been inspected and found to be properly functioning. Tel Nof Air Base.

It's my eighth day in solitary and I feel like the world is closing in on me. An entire vast system out there is laboring to tear apart my stories, while I lie here in my few square feet unable to do a thing.

"I am from the Tel Nof base," I say.

"Which squadron?"

"The 119th."

"You're a regular officer in the air force?"

"No, I am a pilot in the reserves." Aziz and Sayeed get up.

"We must go now. We'll be back later."

Where do they need to go at ten at night? But they're already outside the cell. Sami removes the two chairs and I'm left with *The House at Pooh Corner* inside my cast for the eighth day running and with the knowledge that I must quickly revise my whole story, now that I've moved from Herzliya to Tel Nof.

As time passes, weakness envelops me like a shroud. It's a particularly cold night and I'm shivering inside the cast, uncertain what to expect. Are they coming back? Are they not coming back? I lie wide awake with eyes open, unable to sleep. At around one in the morning, the cell door opens. Sayeed is back—to my relief I must admit, with four guards. They blindfold me, place me on a stretcher and start carrying me to the big room. To my surprise, Sayeed walks beside me.

"You remember that you asked me to tell you when the Americans launched Apollo 12 to the moon?" he asks.

"Sure," I tell him through my blindfold.

"Well, they're on their way to the moon now."

Once my stinking body has been placed back in the bed in the big room, the guards leave. Sami goes out for a moment and I pull *The House at Pooh Corner* out of the cast and try to put it on the bedside table that stands just where it did before. In my haste, my arm bumps into the side of the table and the book falls to the floor. Will the book's sudden appearance on the floor give me away? At this point I don't care. Apollo 12 is on its way to the moon, but I won't get to follow its journey as I pray that it, too, like its predecessor, makes it there and back safely. I don't know who the astronauts are. I only know that I'm intensely jealous of them, burning with the envy of one who always aspired to be at the vanguard of human achievement in the world of aerospace. But I no longer belong to that world. These fantastic things are happening beyond the walls of my prison.

It's mid-November now, more than two months since I was captured. The interrogations still haven't ended and I have to prepare myself for the potential implications of the changes that have occurred in the past week.

The hour is late, but Sami and I both understand that I have returned for another round in the big room, the room reserved just for me in Abbasiya Prison east of Cairo. I pull the sheet down to uncover my upper body and point at my black chest without saying a word. Sami looks me in the eye, nods briefly and leaves the room.

I take the siddur from the bedside table and start going through the prayers that I did not recite during the days in solitary. When I finish praying, I turn to the chapters from *Pirkei Avot*, Ethics of the Fathers that are also in the prayer book. *Anyone whose deeds exceed his wisdom, his wisdom shall endure. And one whose wisdom exceeds his deeds, his wisdom shall not endure.* The pilot performs most of his actions within the narrow confines of the cockpit, all by his lonesome. Much as he may try to tell others about it, he can never truly describe all the moments of great difficulty, effort, and often fear, that occur as he strives to execute the perfect mission, which is his ultimate objective. And captivity means the pilot cannot discuss even the slightest thing that he could otherwise talk about.

I ask myself if up to now my actions have been more abundant than my wisdom. Up to now I have managed to gingerly protect the air force, Ron, Asher, Buki, Salmon, Carmi and all of my other very dear friends. I've protected all that is important to me in my actual professional life—the way we perform dogfights, the systems we have in the Mirage, the ground systems that support us and accompany us whenever the order to "engage" comes over the "Green Radio"—the ground control interception channel, and countless other things that I've been interrogated about.

"I am from the 119th Squadron from the Tel Nof air base" are the first true words I've spoken in two months. Now I must show that not only are my actions abundant but my wisdom as well. I must find a way to keep on protecting that which has given my life such meaning… ever since air force commander Motti Hod pinned flight wings on my chest five and a half years prior to my capture.

The door opens and Sami comes in, lugging a big metal tub that he holds by its two handles. He sets the tub down at the foot of my bed and I can see that it is filled about halfway with steaming water. Then he pulls a towel off his left shoulder, dips it in the water and begins to wash me, starting with my face. After each pass with the damp towel over a small part of my skin, he dips it again in the water, squeezes it out and resumes the cleaning operation. It's been so long since I felt the touch of warm water on my body. The sensation is enchanting, like an encounter with an old friend whose face I've almost forgotten. I lie there without uttering a word, moving my body in response to Sami's indications. Lifting my left shoulder, then my right shoulder, closing my eyes when he passes the towel over my face and lying flat and staring at the ceiling when no movements are required of me. When Sami gets down to about the middle of my chest, he stops and says,

"No more is possible, Captain."

I look down at the tub. The water is blacker than black and is useless now. Sami bends down, picks up the tub of water and leaves the room. I look myself over. My upper body is more or less the natural color of my skin and from mid-chest down, the part that remained untouched by the wet towel is dark as a crow. I'm like some two-toned creature.

I'm thinking that we'll keep on with the cleaning with another tub of water, but Sami comes in and says, "That's enough for tonight. You need to sleep." He spreads his blanket out on the floor, behind the head of my bed, in his usual spot, and I am left alone with my thoughts.

Othman serves me breakfast the next day as if he hadn't just spent the past eight days abusing me in solitary in his nasty way. When he sits down to read the newspaper, I call his name.

"Yes, Captain," he answers.

"Othman, the Americans sent pilots to the moon. Right?"

"Really?" Othman replies with a question. "How do you know?"

"Mr. Sayeed told me last night."

"Let me check." He leafs through the paper, and after a minute he swats it with the back of his hand and says, "Na'am, Captain, the Americans are going to the moon."

"What are the names of the pilots, Othman?"

"Let me check, Captain."

"Othman, there are three pilots," I say, giving him more information. "Find me their names." I'm getting carried away with the idea that I might feel connected to the international community, if only for a fleeting moment.

Othman furrows his brow, and says finally, "The Americans sent only two pilots this time."

"Three, Othman, three," I tell him in my meager Arabic.

He checks again. "Only two, Captain."

"Three," I tell him. "Two will walk on the moon and the third…" Here my Arabic reaches its expressive limits and I make a circular motion with my hand, in an attempt to convey the idea that there is another astronaut who remains in the spaceship and hovers around the moon, waiting for his two comrades.

Othman looks at the newspaper again, and then he looks at me and says in a harsh tone that will brook no further argument, "Two pilots, Captain. Two. That's all!"

The "That's all!" is said so angrily that I give in and say it seems he is right. "What are the names of the two pilots, Othman?"

He opens the paper again, studies it once more with creased brow, closes it, looks straight at me and says: "Two pilots, Captain—One's name is Houston and the other's name is Texas."

So I won't get to be part of the international community that is aware of how the world is changing each morning. Othman will never go beyond his current abilities, which reach their peak when he acts out for me, with utmost seriousness, the movies of Anthony Quinn. And I will remain with all I have left now—to focus on myself and what lies ahead for me. What will happen from here on? How will things develop? What payment will be required of me so that the beatings will stop and I won't be returned to solitary once more?

What I've said already about Tel Nof is doubly disturbing to me—the fact that I spoke the truth, and the fact that I was caught lying. Our personality traits and basic upbringing have a most lasting effect upon us, apparently. Even if lying is an inevitable part of captivity, the discovery of the untruth by the interrogator, by the enemy, and the need to admit it, feels like a diminishment of one's honor, and I believe my captors see it the same way. I am the one who endlessly repeated, "An Israeli pilot never lies," making that declaration an integral component of the complex relationship that was being constructed with my interrogators. And now, this important foundation of my standing has been gravely undermined. To what extent will the exposure of the lie alter the tenor of the interrogations when they resume? How will it affect the delicate balance that has existed up to now among Aziz, Sayeed and me during the questioning? Will the premise that someone who's been caught in one lie must have been lying the whole time now be applied?

Twenty-Four

15-NOV-1969

In the afternoon the door opens, and as expected, in walk Aziz and Sayeed. Aziz wants to know everything about Tel Nof. He's even brought a sketch of the base. The sketch is both accurate and inaccurate. The base's runways have been accurately drawn, but other facilities have been placed way off the mark. We get into a discussion about the base, which in all honesty, being a relatively young pilot, I am not all that familiar with. Aziz wants to know all sorts of crazy things that I know nothing about. Finally, I latch onto a formula. Aziz keeps harping on the number of fuel tankers at the base. He won't accept my claim that I don't know. I haven't bothered to tell him, of course, that unlike the Egyptian Air Force's ground fueling system, which is based on tankers, we have a different method.

By now, after hundreds of hours of questioning, I understand that the Egyptian interrogators assume that our air force is a mirror image of the Egyptian Air Force, with minor differences that they must uncover through their questioning. Aziz returns to the issue of the tankers again and again.

"Forty-three tankers," I finally tell him.

He writes the number down on the sheet of paper in front of him, smiles and says, "You see, there are things that you know and you're not telling." He's right about that—I haven't told him that I am a graduate of Pilot Course Number 43 and that I'm going back to the system of using numbers that have some meaning for me, so I can remember them easily. He keeps on questioning me about Tel Nof, not mentioning even once that I was caught out lying. He stays until the evening and is incredibly friendly. There's a good atmosphere in the room and we even partake of the daily meal to break the Ramadan fast together. He looks like someone who's had a great weight lifted from him. He's disproved the story of the airport in Herzliya, and now he can go to his commanders with a detailed description of the base at Tel Nof.

I can't feel as pleased as he does. Talking about Tel Nof has been agony for me, and I can't stop thinking about Giora Epstein, the "King of the Sky"—Because of that article about him I had to go through all that I went through for the past eight days. In order to restore some of my standing, if only in my own eyes, I keep bringing up personal matters. Aziz may be a superb officer, but the time has come for him to hear my complaints.

For example, I mention the fifty-five days that Dr. Absalem said would have to pass before the cast could be removed from my arm, and tell him they are neglecting my medical care. I repeat my demand to see Boisard. I say it is high time the sheets on my bed were changed. And I even go so far as to say that the Egyptian food is terrible and that since the day I arrived in Egypt I have not had even a single egg to eat.

"Maybe you don't have eggs in Egypt," I add, getting a little carried away in the heat of the moment. This was just before dinnertime, and when the meal comes, lo and behold an egg has been added to the menu—albeit the smallest egg I have ever laid eyes on. Somehow I have the feeling that despite Tel Nof and despite the new avenues of interrogation that have been opened, something is playing in my favor.

After Aziz and Sayeed left, Sayeed came back with another package from Israel. It contained sweets and a few personal items. He gave me two blank Red Cross postcards for me to write, to be sent to Israel, saying he would come to pick them up tomorrow. In the package I found a stick of Old Spice deodorant. Since I still reek, I rub it over most of my body, especially my chest, as far as my cast and physical limitations will allow. I recite the *kriyat shema* bedtime prayer and go to sleep, not quite sure what is going on.

Sayeed reappears the next day. He tells me that soon I will meet the man from the Red Cross. He takes the two postcards that I've written and leaves. In the afternoon, a uniformed Egyptian officer comes into my room. He walks over to my bed, holds up one of my postcards and, pointing to it, asks me in Hebrew what I meant to write in a certain place. This was the postcard to Miriam, in which I wrote that the deodorant was an excellent idea. I explain to him what it says. Satisfied, he tells me that they thought the line about the deodorant was some kind of secret code, and then he wishes me well. The whole thing is so surreal it feels like a scene straight out of *The House at Pooh Corner*.

In the evening I am taken to the hospital in Al-Maadi. It seems clear that another meeting with Boisard is finally going to take place. I am put through the usual appearance upgrades— bathing and a haircut. I am taken down to the lowest floor, where the remainder of the cast is sawed off my left arm. My withered arm is completely exposed now. But to my great shock and dismay, even without the cast I cannot bend it at the elbow. The arm is stuck at a ninety-degree angle, and there is no one I can consult with about the odds of altering its fate. For the first time, I can see just where the elbow was broken and where the surgical incision was sewn up. Strangest of all is the being able to feel the screw that was inserted along the elbow, and because of the scrawniness of the arm is protruding from either side of the joint. At the end of the day, I am lying in the comfortable hospital bed, secretly hoping that maybe Nadia will be the shift nurse, knowing that tomorrow I will meet with a representative of the outside world, and stroking my poor, mangled arm.

Nadia does not appear, but Boisard does arrive the next day, this time without the whole army of media people that accompanied him on his first visit. I am seething with anger.

"Where were you for more than a month?" I berate him. "You said you would come to see me more often than that."

"They wouldn't let me see you. I kept requesting another meeting and they wouldn't agree," he replies in a somewhat apologetic tone.

I tell him about the terrible month I've endured, and that it was ten times worse because I wrongly believed that here in Cairo there was someone who was meant to protect me. He apologizes again, gives me regards from Israel and hands me a bundle of letters. He tells me about the efforts to arrange a prisoner swap—but only about the Foreign Ministry's actions. I ask him if my postcards from the first visit made it to Israel. Not all of them, he tells me.

We spend about half an hour together. It's not like the first meeting, but it's good, very good even. I still remember the blows I received from the Sudanese giant and, as I ponder it, captivity feels at once excruciatingly slow and dizzyingly fast like a rollercoaster. There I was in the solitary dungeon, praying aloud to God, pleading with him to help me before total despair set in. And not so many days later, here I am in the hospital, clean and perfectly trimmed and shaved, and with my left arm freed from the plaster cast.

I write another five postcards to send to Israel. The postcards to Miriam and my parents are nearly identical in content. And I go so far as to apologize, given Boisard's report that not all of the postcards made it to Israel, that I am writing identical postcards. If the Egyptian military wants to keep one postcard in its museum, I explain, then the second postcard will fill in what's missing.

In the evening I am returned to my room in the prison. The prayer book and the other books are waiting for me on the bedside table, just where I left them, but my package—the one I received from the Red Cross prior to leaving for the hospital, is gone. The next day, as usual, I don't eat the entire breakfast, but leave some on the tray on the bedside table to eat later. Othman comes to take the tray and turns to go.

"Hey, wait, Othman, I haven't finished yet."

"What you ate, Captain, is enough. You need to finish it all at once."

I think of this as just another one of Othman's whims, and go on with the day as usual, asking myself in which chapter of my life in captivity I am now. At noon I receive a meal that is much smaller than normal. I figure it has to do somehow with the Ramadan fast. Again I place the bit I haven't finished on the bedside table. Othman comes in and takes the tray away. I start to suspect that although Othman is a devout Muslim, he is occasionally helping himself to some of my food in order to ease the fast. But by the evening I grasp that there's a new pattern of behavior here. When Sami relieves Othman, he tells me that according to the new orders, I am not allowed to save food. I tell Sami that I wish to meet with Sayeed, and I start to feel hungry. The next day my hunger only grows. When I get to the end of lunch, I collect all the remaining rice, put it in the two pita-quarters on the tray and hide them under the pillow. Later on, when I'm hungry and when Othman has left the room, I can pull out a piece of pita with rice from under the pillow, pull the sheet over my head and furtively eat the leftovers from lunch. But much as I come up with tricks to hide food between the folds of my bed linen, the shrinking quantities just heighten my appetite. Before long, hunger is the only thing on my mind.

Sayeed does not appear on the second day, or the third day, or the fourth or fifth day, and meanwhile I am getting hungrier and hungrier. The main thing is—I just cannot understand what this is all about. If it's meant to be a pressure tactic, they could have easily just sent me back to solitary. And if it's in preparation for further interrogation, then why aren't they coming to question me? If they think that I lied, then what is keeping them from demanding that I tell the truth? The hunger is steadily driving me mad. All I can think about is food, and I vow that when I get back to Israel I will only eat in fancy restaurants.

In the evenings, I search for grains of rice that may have fallen and gotten scattered in the sheets, and when I find one or two, they are more precious to me than gold. In an almost primitive way, the whole situation provokes in me a tremendous fury at, not to say hatred for, Othman and even Sami. In unrestrained outbursts, I return to the technique of ranting loudly in Hebrew with a menacing tone and expression. I unburden myself of all my pent-up feelings. I shout at them, I curse them and their families, I give elaborate speeches in which I pour out my heart. And they are quite discombobulated to be on the receiving end of these rants.

Othman gives me threatening looks, and when I keep right on, he walks out of the room—apparently to keep from losing control and resorting to violence. The second night that I shout at Sami in Hebrew, he rushes at my bed, grabs the sheets of writing paper from the bedside table and rips them to pieces.

He threatens to report me to his superiors, and I yell right back at him, "Go ahead and report it, you fucker!" among other such linguistic pearls. After a few minutes of yelling, I calm down, lie back in bed and dream about Aunt Leah's roadside restaurant in Gedera where we would always go to eat a good steak after night flights.

The starvation process is entering its sixth day when the door opens and in walks Sayeed. Once again I've been manipulated into feeling weak, exhausted and, as always, cut off from any information that could help me decipher the reality around me.

"What's going on?" I ask Sayeed. "Why won't you let a POW eat?"

"You cannot insult the Egyptian military, Captain," he answers tersely.

"I insulted the Egyptian military?"

"Yes—you wrote that the Egyptian military wants to keep your postcards in its museum."

"Sayeed," I tell him, "I only said that because not all the postcards that I wrote during the first meeting with Boisard were delivered to my family in Israel, and besides, you know that I tend to joke around sometimes."

"So don't joke around anymore about the Egyptian military. It is a glorious military and it will not tolerate any such thing."

"Okay, Sayeed, I get it. But how much longer do you all intend to keep on starving me?"

"Starting today, you'll get as much food as you were getting before you insulted us."

In the evening, Sami comes in and brings me dinner. For the first time since arriving in prison I receive a meal that is not the usual fare. On the plate is a baked fish with fried tomatoes, fried onion and potatoes. "What's this?" I say to Sami. He answers me in Arabic.

"This is fish from the Nile, from our river." I eat the fish, but I'm still hungry. I'm hoping that, starting tomorrow, I will build up my body again. My torso is all withered, and a big gap has opened up between it and the plaster cast around it. My arms have become emaciated too. I recite the Grace after Meals over the fish from the Nile, just as I have been doing after every meal, even if it didn't include bread. I pick up Agnon's *A Simple Story* and start to read it again.

Twenty-Five

29-NOV-1969

I know that this morning I am starting another day of nothing. It's Saturday. For a few days now, things have been different than "old times." People I've never laid eyes on before are coming into my room and chatting with me. The conversation is not hostile. Not unfriendly. Certainly not threatening. My best guess is that they are middle-echelon officers, even though all of them are in civilian dress. All restrictions appear to have been lifted, and anyone who can do so is coming to my room for a direct encounter with an Israeli pilot.

I do not interpret this to mean that a prisoner exchange deal is imminent. Optimism would be too cheap. Even the fact that Aziz hasn't come to interrogate me for the past ten days is not making me feel any better. It's the whole experience of captivity, not just the interrogation sessions that is steadily crushing me, destroying me bit by bit. It's the realization—

having already seen the wretched condition of my left arm after the cast was removed—that I am also about to lose my right leg, if not to amputation then to permanent severe disability. It's the physical price that captivity is going to exact from me, which is becoming more and more real and frightening. It's the need that's been tearing me to pieces to speak Hebrew with someone, with someone who is a friend, with someone whose counsel I could seek. And above all, it's the knowledge that as long as I am in Egypt I am absolutely helpless. I am like clay in the hands of the potter, in the hands of my captors. I am careful, therefore, not to build up expectations, since I know all too well that the fall I will experience when they are disappointed will be painful. Very painful.

People tend to think that the hardest part of being a POW is the physical torture. They are mistaken. As awful as it may be, such torture at least has a beginning, a middle and eventually, a recovery. The loneliness, the humiliation, the total uncertainty, the endless separation from the rest of the world, the end-date of captivity that only seems to recede further with each passing day—these are the things that gradually crush your very essence. These are the things against which you have to muster every ounce of mental and emotional strength.

I am living in a monotonous daily routine that just heightens the frustration. Running through each day is the sliver of hope that any moment now the door will open and something will happen. But the days are indistinguishable from one another and I am sinking into an ever-deepening melancholy.

Two days ago, in the evening, I had a visit from two men I'd never seen before. They spoke to me pleasantly, and expressed their great admiration for me. They believed, so they said, that it would be best for both countries' sake if we maintained contact once I finally returned to Israel. Occasional reports from me would enable them to do what was needed so that one day the hostility between Egypt and Israel would dissipate. I don't remember just how this sort of thing looks in the movies, but in real life, when they're trying to recruit you to collaborate with the enemy, it's a bloodcurdling moment. A moment in which you feel a total siege closing in on you. There is no correct response. Anything apart from a firm refusal is akin to betrayal. But on the other hand, an unequivocal "no" may spell the start of another trip down a path I've come to know all too well—of being subjected to various pressure tactics.

I divert the conversation onto the topic of future relations between Israel and Egypt. From there I steer it to "I'm tired" and "Let me sleep on it." When they leave the room, I am highly agitated. Whenever I reach such extremes, the plaster trousers encasing my legs feel like a death trap and I am desperate to be freed from them. The two men do not return again, but the memory of the encounter with them continues to hover in the room.

The big advantage of Saturday, the Jewish Sabbath, is that because of the sanctity of the day, I know there is no chance of anything significant happening in regard to a possible prisoner swap. And so I can pass the time reading and sneaking games of checkers with myself.

Twenty-Six

6-DEC-1969

The door opens very early in the morning and in comes the little prison barber. His expression is blank, as usual. Under Sami's watchful eye, he takes the leather strop from his small case, hones the blade on it and proceeds to give me a perfect shave. As the barber leaves, another man I don't recognize enters the room. And for the first time since I came to Egypt, someone inserts his hand inside my cast and rummages all over, searching to see if I've hidden anything inside it. He does not find anything, including the folded-up chess board, which is kept inside a special hiding place I gradually constructed deep inside the plaster covering my left thigh.

While I am eating my breakfast, I hear some sort of vehicle maneuvering outside the door to the room. I finish drinking the tea. Soldiers come in, transfer me to a stretcher and carry me outside. Before me I see the open rear doors of an Egyptian military ambulance. I am laid on the floor of the ambulance and beside me I find Nissim Ashkenazi.

We are lying in opposite directions. My feet are facing forward, towards the front of the vehicle, while Nissim, who is lying on his back, has his head toward the front. The doors of the ambulance close and it starts to move. Sami does not say goodbye to me. Actually, no one at all bids me goodbye. I wonder whether I am now being put through some other exercise that is designed to break me.

But I am in an ambulance, I am not blindfolded and I lift my head to look at Nissim. He too lifts his head, holds out his hand and says, "Nissim Ashkenazi." I shake his hand, reply, "Giora Romm," and lay my head back down on the stretcher.

The ambulance winds its way out of the prison and when it gets on to the main road, I gather the strength to start whistling the tune to the famous Six Day War song "We've Come for Reserve Duty." With the back of his right hand, Nissim lightly presses on my hand. I inquire about his condition and am surprised to learn that his injuries are quite similar to mine, though a bit more serious. He tells me that he underwent more surgery on his arm just a few days ago and that it hurts. Sitting on the bench next to him is his Sayeed, a pleasant-looking fellow who appears to have much sympathy for Nissim. My Sayeed sits next to me and doesn't say a word. No one in the ambulance is speaking, and the only clue that we are headed east, in the direction of the Suez Canal, is the sun that is always shining through the front windshield. But I refrain from sharing this observation with anyone. The journey continues in near total silence, apart from a few words about adjusting the position in which the ailing Nissim is lying, a subject that falls under the responsibility of his Sayeed.

The mood in the ambulance is not one of relief or excitement, and surely not joy. Each passenger is alone with his thoughts, brooding, each for his own reasons. My reason is that I am still of little faith. The long months of utter darkness about my situation have made me wary, not to say fearful, and I view everything as another move intended to weaken my much-depleted emotional support system even further.

But the ambulance keeps driving in the direction of the rising sun, and now it wends its way through the streets of what looks to be a partially destroyed city. We are unloaded from the ambulance and placed on the ground, and within a few minutes, Nissim disappears.

I remain alone with Sayeed, who for reasons unknown to me has lapsed into total silence. I lie there for ten minutes, twenty minutes, thirty minutes… The time keeps passing and it's clear to me that something has gone wrong. Boisard appears. He is the first one who talks to me. Nissim and I are being exchanged for seventy-two Egyptian POWs. Thirty-six Egyptians have already crossed back into their country, and Nissim has crossed back to our side. And now they can't solve the riddle of how to carry out the second half of the deal, as there is only a single ship. Who will be the last to cross over, the Egyptians or me?

The lack of trust between the two countries is total, and I can already see myself being transported back to Cairo because the circle hasn't been squared. Deep down I know that if at the end of the day I find myself in an ambulance heading back to Cairo because they couldn't manage to work out the problem of the ship, it will be more than I can bear. Outwardly, as usual, I am able to maintain restraint. I am lying on the floor of a bombed out building that is otherwise completely nondescript. The walls are scarred and pockmarked, and like always, I haven't the faintest idea what is happening even thirty feet away.

An Egyptian officer comes in and kneels down beside me. He tells me that he is a doctor and asks how I'm feeling. To me he looks just like a combat officer trying to pass himself off as a doctor. I ask him to tell me what barotitis is—the only medical term I remember from the pilots' course. He gives me a very precise answer, explaining that the condition occurs when a plane makes a steep descent and pressure is trapped in the skull when the Eustachian tubes are not clear. He is a doctor, no question about it. I feel embarrassed about my error in judgment.

"You've covered me in a ratty blanket that's all sandy," I tell him.

"We got this blanket from you, Captain," he says, showing me the Hebrew letters printed on the far edge. I'm feeling restless and repeatedly chastened by the kind Egyptian medical officer. And I'm furious that our people haven't bothered to provide the best supplies to take care of me, to uphold the dignity of the military.

"Just a little more patience and everything will work out," the doctor says to me. And right then, as if on cue, from the other side of the wrecked wall comes a man in a white suit.

"I am one of the Red Cross representatives in Israel," he says to me in English. I can't believe my eyes. I recognize him! Miriam and I were sitting one Saturday afternoon at the California Restaurant on Frishman Street in Tel Aviv, and this fellow was sitting at the table next to us, in his white suit. He was a very handsome man and the two of us couldn't help noticing him and his gorgeous female companion, and thinking how different they looked, with their style of dress and their blondness, from the locals.

"I know you from California," I say to him, surprising myself.

"I've never been to California," he replies immediately.

"Not California in America, the California Restaurant in Tel Aviv," I explain.

He looks at me in astonishment and says, "Well, I've come to take you back. It's about time that you went back there."

And then Sayeed and a few more soldiers appear behind him. They hoist the stretcher, and we depart the ruined building where I've lain for about three hours. Ahead of me I see the Suez Canal and a small ship docked there. Before they put me on the ship they stop.

Sayeed holds out his hand. He is quite emotional. I've never seen him like this. The right corner of his mouth is trembling uncontrollably.

"It was an honor to know you, Captain," he says in English. I look at him. I want to say something but the words get stuck in my throat.

"May God be with you," he adds in Arabic, and then he turns around and walks away.

Twenty-Seven

6-DEC-1969

On Saturday, December 6, 1969, the 26th of Kislev in the year 5630 on the Hebrew calendar, the second day of Hanukkah, I cross the Suez Canal from west to east on the deck of a small Egyptian ship. I lay on a stretcher, covered with a sand-encrusted woolen army blanket, and watch as the eastern bank of the canal looms ever closer. My legs are encased in a trouser-shaped plaster cast and my hands lay atop my body. As if to hide it, my right hand covers my left, which is withered to almost half the size and stuck at a right angle with no mobility in the elbow.

In the distance I can make out a group of people watching me from the banks of the canal. The group is khaki-colored, and I imagine they are reservists who happen to get the chance to observe the unusual event of a prisoner swap. The ruins of Qantara—where I'd been held for three hours while the Red Cross tried to solve the riddle of how the prisoner exchange would proceed with just a single ship—fade into the distance as the ship begins maneuvering towards the eastern bank. Four Egyptian sailors in colorful woolen caps lift the stretcher and carefully pass it over the strip of water between the boat and shore to four Israeli soldiers.

I gaze silently at the cluster of unfamiliar Israelis, breathing in my first moments on Israeli soil. The group parts and Motti Hod, the air force commander, steps forward. Next to him stands a smiling Yak Nevo, commander of the Hatzor base where the air force's first Phantom squadron had been established. I would have been one of its first pilots had I not been summoned on September 11 to my Mirage squadron and set out on the interceptor flight from which I was only now returning, three months later.

"Welcome home," Motti says to me, and shakes my hand.

"Hello Motti, Hello Yak," I answer softly, looking around and trying to adjust to the stark change in my surroundings.

Motti is dressed in plain khaki without any military ranks or insignia, and a pistol is attached to his belt. My thoughts wander for a moment to Anwar in his perfectly pressed khaki uniform, also devoid of any insignia. From out of nowhere, an authoritative voice gives an order to get moving, and quickly, to get out of here, as if some danger still lurks. The group hurries along, with my stretcher being carried at the front. A green military ambulance waiting down the road swallows me up. Carefully and without saying a word, the soldiers set down the stretcher in the designated spot and exit the vehicle.

Motti enters through the rear door and closes it behind him. "I'm glad you're here with us, we worked very hard on it."

I say nothing.

"So how was it for you, Giora?" My silence is making Motti a little nervous.

"You have no idea how hard it was, Motti," I finally say. More silence in the ambulance. "You have nothing to worry about as far as the interrogations are concerned, they don't know anything about us," I add.

"That's not important now, Giora. Are you okay? What's important to me now is that you're okay."

"I'll be okay, Motti. I'll be fine." I notice, to my surprise, I am speaking Hebrew with an American accent, especially in the way I pronounce the letter *resh*. Apparently it won't be that easy to erase the traces of the last three months in which I spoke only English.

Motti pats me gently on the shoulder and leaves, and the ambulance gets going.

Just ten minutes later I am inside an air force Super Perlon helicopter. Nissim Ashkenazi who'd been in captivity the whole time that I was, and a little longer, lay on the upper bunk affixed to the right side of the helicopter. He'd undergone another surgery a few days before the prisoner exchange, and it is clear from his face that he is still in pain. After takeoff, one of the other passengers brings over a tray with *sufganiyot*, the traditional Hanukkah jelly donuts. I gape at the tray in astonishment.

"You know that it's Hanukah now, right?"

"No, I don't know." All the others fell silent and regard us awkwardly as if we are two aliens from another galaxy. No one knows how to act around us. I pick up a jelly donut, so different from the pita with salty cheese that had been my daily fare for the past three months. When I raise my head a bit, I notice a newspaper at the end of the bench. I ask to see it and am soon completely absorbed in reading it, not skipping a word, trying to reconnect with a world that is more remote from me than the other passengers could ever comprehend.

A big crowd is waiting when we land at Tel Hashomer Hospital.

Miriam is here, my mother and father, my two brothers Uri and Amikam, Defense Minister Moshe Dayan, the chief of staff, the head of military intelligence, various air force personnel and lots of people who've come after hearing reports on the radio about the prisoner exchange. Everyone treats me very gingerly, since psychologists have been explaining to them for months that the experience gained from Korean War POWs showed that people who return from captivity are detached from their surroundings, want to keep to themselves, have trouble communicating, and must be handled with great patience and delicacy. Not having read these studies myself, I am excited to see everyone who comes up to my stretcher that has been placed on a hospital gurney in the center of the landing area.

Aside from two hours of medical procedures and examinations conducted by the men who will be my doctors for years to follow—Dr. Farrin, Dr. Horoshovsky and Dr. Yoel Engel—I am surrounded by people all the time. The stream of visitors never stops and every one of them causes me much excitement because they are another dot that I can connect to others in an effort to redraw my previous life.

Around midnight, when it comes time to send away all the well-wishers and to calm down from the reunion, I ask Miriam to stay with me for a few more minutes. The room, at the end of Pavilion 19 of the old Tel Hashomer Hospital, is now quiet and empty. It is just the two of us there, alone. Miriam stands close to my bed and looks nervous in anticipation of what I am about to say.

"I hope that from here on out things will just keep getting better from day to day," I say to her. "I am fairly certain that the human mind will gradually erase the things it is not prepared to take with it forever." Miriam regards me somewhat warily as she listens to my opening words. I notice that she has two lovely braids that she has grown in my absence. They are so different from the way she wore her hair before, and it just drives home to me how much everything can change when you're not around. "So remember what I'm telling you now, before the erasure process gathers steam, because you are my companion for life. Nothing in the world is as hard or as rotten as captivity." In the 119th Squadron, my squadron, "something rotten" was a synonym for "a thorny, very difficult to solve problem."

"If, in the future, my captivity becomes blurred in my mind and my consciousness, always remember what I'm telling you now. Captivity is a horrible nightmare. I hope I'll come out of it."

Miriam kisses me. "You'll come out of it, Giora," she says. "You'll come out of it. Everyone is here with you." She has a basic faith that I will come out of anything. She looks me over one more time and leaves to go home.

I lay here awake for hours, unable to fall asleep, trying to take in the fact that I began the day in the Abbasiya prison on the outskirts of Cairo and am ending it here in Tel Hashomer Hospital on the outskirts of Tel Aviv.

Twenty-Eight

25-JAN-70

I'm walking in the dunes that connect El Arish with Rafah in the Gaza Strip region. I'm advancing pretty quickly, but try as I might to quicken my pace the people about a quarter of a mile behind me are steadily closing the gap. I'm walking in an arc, aiming to skirt the densely populated areas of the Gaza Strip from the east.

Ahead of me I can see small clusters of houses in the dunes among the palm trees, and shadowy figures are moving about amidst the dwellings. My brain is feverishly trying to calculate the odds of being able to get past these figures without having them start pursuing me too. I can't count on passing as an Arab because I don't speak Arabic. Although I'm in civilian clothing that doesn't necessarily give me away as an Israeli, it's not the style of dress that's normally seen around here.

It's getting harder to run and I'm panting more heavily.

I pass by a number of figures who are standing in bunches. Their features are blurry but I can tell that they're staring at me, though they do nothing to try to stop me. This gives me hope that perhaps I will be able to make it to my destination, though I'm not even sure what it is. When I glance behind me, I see that my pursuers are closing the distance and pointing at me. The first light of day is dawning and the idea that darkness might provide me with cover has to be discarded.

My breathing is getting faster and shallower, for the dunes have become more like quicksand and my fear of my pursuers is growing. Ahead I can see scattered bright lights that are gradually being extinguished—the nighttime lights of what I take to be an Israeli village. I desperately hope that I can make it there. I feel intensely jealous of the people who are sleeping there in their homes, safe and sound, at what seems like an unbridgeable distance from me. The knowledge that they are free from any life-and-death worries right now only deepens my sense of my misfortune, the origins of which I can't manage to recall.

The morning mist suddenly clears, and I can distinctly see the barbed wire that separates the Egyptian side from the Israeli side. I can't see any solution to the riddle of how to overcome this obstacle. I start dashing left and right at an ever faster speed. I know I'm about to be caught and I have no plan for how to keep going.

I've reached a dead end. The end of a narrow alley from which there is no exit. This is where all hope runs out...

I wake up. I'm shuddering with fright, my breathing is labored, my forehead is dripping with sweat, my heart is thumping so hard I'm sure the noise will wake Miriam who is sleeping to my left. The early morning sun is starting to filter through the curtains of our bedroom window in the family housing quarters at Hatzor Airbase, and I know that I won't fall back asleep.

I can't get out of bed. Both of my legs are encased in a trousers-shaped cast (the notorious Spica). I've been lying in bed at home for a month now, waiting for another three months to pass until the doctors from Pavilion 17 at Tel Hashomer Hospital are able to see if they were successful in rebuilding my right thigh.

I haven't had any dreams like this since I returned to Israel, and I want to understand its meaning. On the face of it, it's not that complicated, but I just don't get why this dream should suddenly appear now. After all, I'm in no danger nor do I expect to be in any danger in the foreseeable future. What do I have to run away from? Why should I be a hunted person? Why should I fear recapture? No one is after me, and since my return I've been surrounded by as many loving family members and friends as I can possibly handle. And now all of a sudden comes this nightmare. I chalk it up to some trace of the POW experience still occupying a small corner of my brain and assume that it, too, will be washed away as I continue to recover. Basically, I am confident that I have put captivity behind me, in every sense of the word. Right now I need to apply my energies to physical recovery.

The operation to save my thigh was no minor procedure.

The cast that Dr. Absalem had fashioned for me in Egypt was worthless. The fracture was not what they call a clean or simple one. The thigh bone was completely shattered into tiny pieces. After these bone slivers were removed, the famed quadriceps muscle rested on an untethered bone that was about four inches short.

The team of orthopedists at Tel Hashomer Hospital had to reopen the right side of my thigh all the way from my hip to my knee. A seventeen-inch stainless steel nail was inserted and bone was taken from the left side of my pelvis and implanted around the nail. Its natural growth was supposed to serve as the basis for reconstructing the thigh.

Once again I was stuck in plaster trousers. Once again I was immobilized. But this time, when the ambulance took me away from the hospital, it wasn't to solitary confinement in prison, but to my new home in Hatzor. And there Miriam and my own bed awaited me. An iron frame built by technicians from the Hatzor maintenance squadron had been installed above the bed, with a dangling handle that enabled me to hoist myself up without the aid of Sami or Othman.

The Nadia and Aisha of the hospital's Pavilion 17 were called Anka, Gila and Shoshi, and to my delight, they spoke Hebrew. Although they knew nothing of the map on display at the Knesset showing a massive Israel stretching from the Nile to the Euphrates, they and the rest of the medical team got me through the post-surgery pain and the fever that kept returning night after night, and helped me adjust to my severely limited mobility—which was quite similar to what I experienced in Egypt. It was thanks to them that I could eventually return home—to Miriam and to our little sanctuary that she had labored over and lovingly prepared while I was gone.

Miriam wakes up and is surprised to find me lying there awake staring at the ceiling. I don't tell her anything about the dream. I've been up for half an hour already. I'm still upset from the dream and have yet to fully take it in. I don't want to talk about it. I'm hoping it was a one-time event and I would prefer to keep the whole thing to myself.

We start the daily routine. Like every morning, Miriam devotedly performs the chores that were performed by the nurses in the hospital, and when she opens the curtain of the east-facing window, the sun fills the room and the last wisps of the dream vanish. It's nothing more than a scratch on a record that's forgotten as soon as the needle moves on.

Three nights later I find myself running down the corridor of an unfamiliar building. No one is chasing me, but I'm desperate to get out of this place. The more I run, the narrower the corridor becomes, and whenever I follow its curve right or left, the walls close in on me even more. My heart is pounding from the effort of trying to reach an exit before the corridor becomes too narrow to contain me, but the walls just keep inching nearer. It gets so narrow that when I decide to turn around and go back to the mysterious starting point of this race, I can no longer do so. I realize that I am in a dead-end trap...

And again I wake up, completely unnerved by the tight spot to which I was led. The bedroom is pitch dark. I reach out to the right, to the bedside table, and pick up my watch. It's two in the morning. I lie there unmoving, praying that Miriam won't wake up, trying to find a way to calm myself, to let the perspiration dry, to let my heartbeat return to normal, to get my rapid breathing under control, and to try to fall back asleep. A long time passes before I can doze off again, and meanwhile, the understanding begins to sink in that captivity is something that stays with you even when you are not physically there anymore. When I awake again later in the morning, I wonder if this is going to keep happening in the nights to come, and if so, just where these dreams are leading me.

Twenty-Nine

Jan-Apr-1970

The recovery process for a former POW is no different than for anyone else. The bones are the same bones. The muscles are the same muscles. Time's healing effect is the same, and the doctors and nurses do their best either way. And yet, the understanding was slowly sinking in that I was going to pay a physical price for the fact that my real medical treatment only began four months after I was injured.

But the fanfare of my return to Israel overshadowed all else, including the knowledge that I would never again be the same as I was before my capture. My return was a national event. It was a source of great joy for the entire public, in the simplest and purest sense. From my immediate perspective, it meant an endless stream of visitors, some who knew me and others I'd never met before, who came to express their feelings. IDF Chief of Staff Haim Bar-Lev brought me a copy of famed Israeli commando Meir Har-Zion's newly published book. Settlement pioneer Avraham Herzfeld, whom I'd heard of but never met, came to see me and left me a book about the Hashomer Hatzair youth movement. Chief Rabbi Shlomo Goren brought a beautiful menorah for "the descendant of the Hasmoneans." The Red Cross representative in Israel presented me with a book about the history of the Red Cross. IDF Military Intelligence Chief Aharon ("Ahrale") Yariv and the national police commissioner also paid me a visit. Even Prime Minister Golda Meir sat in my room one day and sought to understand my experience. In short, there was nonstop visitor traffic from morning till evening, which left me weary and in need of some quiet and some control over my personal space.

Among the visitors were people from the IDF's Intelligence Branch who came to find out about the interrogations to which I'd been subjected. Speaking to them gave me a real boost because for the first time I was really able to talk about what I'd been through in the months that I was gone. More than anything else, being able to unburden myself—in a very detailed, orderly and systematic way—of all those long nights with Aziz made me feel connected to my Israeliness and to the person I was before all this happened. It was just another version of the post-operation debriefing, an inseparable part of the rhythm to which I'd grown accustomed ever since I became a pilot. It felt good to be an active participant in this sort of thing again. When it was over, I felt lighter and freer.

I spent three more months in bed at home in Hatzor until the Spica was removed and my body was revealed to me in all its wretched glory: skinny and weak legs, an arm that was still completely stuck at a ninety-degree angle, and the overall physical strength of a small child. The medical team was not the least bit perturbed by this, however. For one thing, physical therapy had yet to work its magic on me.

Second, the War of Attrition had filled Pavilion 17 and the adjacent Pavilion 20 with an influx of wounded men who, objectively speaking, were physically worse off than me. After its Six Day Campaign from June 5 to June 10, 1967, when it seized the Sinai Peninsula, the Golan Heights, Gaza Strip, and the West Bank, Israel had increased in size three times over. It now had more than a million Arab "citizens" inside her new borders. Needless to say, the situation was tenuous.

The War of Attrition soon followed. Egypt resolved to take back the Sinai and re-engaged Israel in and around the Suez Canal, the waterway that connects the Mediterranean with the Red Sea and links up with the Indian Ocean. The canal, which is only about 200 yards wide, marked the border between Israel and Egypt in those years. It had been closed to the passage of ships immediately after the Six Day War.

Each country deployed parts of its military on its side of the canal, and at Egypt's instigation, exchanges of gunfire began. The basic goal was to inflict enough casualties among the other side's troops to eventually wear down the leaders and prompt a change in the situation. The war spread to the air as well and Israel made extensive use of its air force. My Mirage was shot down on September 11, 1969, after I'd been called on to respond to an Egyptian MiG-21 attack on Israeli ground positions in the Sinai. The war gradually drew in the world's two superpowers, the United States and the Soviet Union. The world was not pleased that instead of supporting commerce, the canal was a battlefield. American involvement took the form of supplying increasingly sophisticated military technology to Israel. The Soviet Union went further and stationed military forces in Egypt that took part in the fighting.

It was perhaps not the best time to discuss with my doctors the possibility of my returning to flying so soon after being liberated from my plaster trousers and my arm still stuck at ninety degrees. My inquiry evoked raised eyebrows and suggestions that I should be sent for therapy at another section of the hospital—and not an orthopedic one. The thought that I would eventually get back to flying may have been a way of holding on to something familiar now that my world had changed beyond all recognition.

Up to age twenty-four, I'd always controlled my own fate, and now suddenly I was chained to circumstances in all of my decision-making, or to be more accurate, I was forced to let circumstances dictate everything for me. The physical debilitation was the less worrisome part. I would let the doctors and my natural physical ability—which I owed to my parents and to years of strenuous fitness training at my military boarding school in Haifa—take care of that. But there was still the profound emotional impact to contend with. The euphoria surrounding my return to Israel had initially dwarfed any concerns about my future, but it could no longer obscure the turbulent state of my psyche caused by my time in captivity. The unpredictable and untamable dreams were just one sign of this new turmoil.

The more rational parts of my brain also understood that I'd been maneuvered to a new crossroads in my life, an unmarked crossroads. I would have to keep on forging my path as I had done up to now, but with many more constraints, some of which were not yet fully revealed. Returning to flying was an anchor that, deep down, I clung to with all my might.

Psychologists from the air force medical corps had already been to see me. They were civilian IDF employees, dressed in typically disheveled Israeli style, and very pleasant to talk to. The leader of the group was a most impressive man from Kibbutz Palmahim, whose name I do not recall. He spent many hours with me in my room in Tel Hashomer Hospital, in the period following my surgery. He came to size me up and to see just what sort of creature had come back from Egypt. And keen as he was to treat me, he was obviously just as eager to hear my tales from captivity. At the time, the literature describing former POWs from the Korean War was the sole basis psychologists had for understanding the mental state of freed captives. His curiosity derived from his desire to set aside this conventional wisdom. He was a person who inspired trust, and I opened up to him as much as I possibly could. I laid out the chronology of my captivity for him, analyzed the various ways in which pressure was exerted upon me and, finally, shared with him my conclusions as a reluctant expert on the subject. He related what I told him to the known behavior patterns of the human mind, and provided my story with a scientific interpretation.

When we finished our series of sessions, the psychologist had the look of someone who'd come upon a great treasure. He'd filled several notebooks with neat, dense handwriting and planned, I presume, to update the air force's psychological staff to be ready to treat any future ex-POWs, should the need arise. For my part, I understood from his explanations that I'd gone and gotten myself a lifelong trauma. An incurable kind of trauma.

Incurable? Well, not exactly, but one for which there was no set method or any systematic medical-psychological procedure to smooth over the scars that had been etched in the psyche. In any event, there is no way for the ex-POW to erase all traces of his captivity.

Again I was left all alone to pass the long nights at the hospital thinking about how to try to carry on with my life from this point forward. There may have been many alternatives, as people like to say these days, but out of all of them, I knew, not necessarily rationally, but rather intuitively, that the best medicine for these scars was called a Mirage. A genuine appreciation of just what this "medicine" and its side effects entailed was still far beyond me at that point. But it was vitally important to me to set a goal for myself, a quite lofty one as usual, to guide my actions in the time ahead.

Thirty

Apr-Jul-1970

Shoshi—the Israeli Nadia—spends many hours at my bedside after the Pavilion has closed to visitors and is a good listener and sounding board. Unlike the other nurses, she is a nurse officer in active IDF duty, and this serves as the basis for the closeness and trust between us—the kind that arises from the proximity of two young professionals serving in the IDF, each in his respective field.

I often spend the evenings in a wheelchair outside Pavilion 17. From here I have a view of the section of highway south of the Mesubim Junction, to the east of the high mound formed by the Hiriya landfill. Cars are traveling in both directions and I am acutely aware that inside them are people who have the great privilege of enjoying a normal life each day anew.

And meanwhile here I am, having spent the last eight months of my life supine and immobile and idle, in one room or another, in one bed or another, and some of that time on bare concrete. I still have no clear plan of action for my future, but amid this haze a few points of light have begun to emerge, and I hope I will be able to navigate by them. They all revolve around the effort to get my life back to the place where it changed so drastically and to continue afresh down the path I started out on.

The dreams keep visiting me at irregular intervals, sometimes once a week, sometimes once every two weeks. And always with one of two fixed motifs—a predicament in which I am about to fall into the hands of pursuers (their identity isn't quite clear yet I know with utter certainty that when I am caught it will be very bad), or a predicament in which I find myself in an extremely tight space that just keeps getting smaller. And what follows is always the same too: I wake up with a start, labor to get all the physical symptoms under control, and go back to sleep. To the dreams' credit, I must say that whenever one does visit, it does not make a return appearance later that same night. But they are scary and exhausting. Each time I am being chased in a different landscape, under different circumstances. Some of these landscapes remain vivid in my mind for a long time afterwards.

Miriam knows all about the dreams now but she has a very firm view about my mental vigor. She believes that I've returned from the mysterious experience of captivity even stronger than before and with an even keener appetite for life and action, and she is a strong and faithful source of support.

Out in the world, the War of Attrition is raging. Israel has never known such a brutal war, or a war that feels so remote from the home front. It's as if two separate nations are living side by side—the State of Israel and another state located in the Suez Canal sector. Two parts of the same flesh that are completely estranged from one another. My prism is that of the goings-on at Hatzor Airbase, an atypical place where life ostensibly goes on as normal in the State of Israel, but for which a significant portion of daily activity is actually occurring in the State of the Suez Canal. Pilots come to visit me at home in the evenings, and they tell me about what's happening on the base and what the mood is. I can't help but admire the pilots and navigators of the Phantom squadron, which has been entrusted with the bulk of the missions. Tonight I can hear them, in the family lounge that's opposite my room, rehearsing their performance for the upcoming Israel Independence Day air force ball.

I've progressed from the wheelchair to walking with iron crutches that were specially fashioned for my asymmetrical arms. This has finally enabled me to ride in a car, though not as a driver, of course. I've also started to take an interest again in the flight squadrons at Hatzor and I try to catch glimpses of what they're up to. One Saturday I am "standing," leaning on my two crutches, near the takeoff position of Runway 29 at Hatzor. Phantoms are rolling slowly toward takeoff, readying for a mission to strike the Egyptian naval base at Ras Banas, far away in Upper Egypt. Having participated as an observer and listener at the briefing, I know who is under each white helmet that I see from afar in the cockpits. I should have been one of those helmets, guiding the air force's finest plane to its mission.

I was in the first course for Phantom planes. But then, with my own hands, with a mistake that I made—and I have no intention whatsoever of attributing it to anyone else—I brought about this radical shift in my life's direction. I led myself to this point where I am no more than an observer who has to rely on crutches. I stand here leaning on the car, as the Phantoms take off for Ras Banas.

Even after all the takeoffs I have witnessed in my life, I could keep on watching them without end. The power of the engines when they open up. The blow to the ears when the afterburner is activated. The rhythmic build of the plane's acceleration. The elegant motion of the raising of the nose gear followed by the lifting of the plane's nose until it breaks contact with the runway. And finally, the climactic moment when the wheels are retracted and the transition from rolling vehicle to flying creature is complete. Time and again it all culminates in a shiver of excitement that makes the heart skip a beat. To me the process is like an endless replay of a victory over forces that seek to pull you down, hold you back, oppose you, keep you tethered to the ground. The lead Phantom executes a wide right turn followed by a left turn, making a large semi-circle to allow the rest of the planes in the formation to join him. While I remain all alone on the concrete plaza, watching the four planes as they get farther away, trailing plumes of black smoke and already flying in very tight formation, over the Ashkelon area, heading southward. It's clear to me that I'm still very far from being able to fly.

I'm still at the stage where the ambulance from the base is transporting me almost daily to Tel Hashomer Hospital for physical therapy. Adam Weiler, my good friend from the military boarding school, was killed on the banks of the Suez Canal while commanding a tank company. When he fell he joined Nadav Klein, another big star from our class, who was killed nine months earlier on the banks of the Jordan River, and I know that I cannot be like those people who are oblivious to what is happening around the Canal. Ever since I was young, I've seen military service as my calling, and I do not intend to allow my fall into captivity and my injuries to divert me into some other realm, certainly not when the country is at war and when all of my dearest friends are out there fighting, each with his own unit.

As summer approaches I solidify my plans. I will study economics at the university. This will enable me to undergo medical treatments during the school breaks until my physical disability is no longer an obstacle to getting back to flying. By now I'm only using a cane, so I come up with a new idea. The Mirage may still be a plane that I can only look at, but a Cessna? A Cessna I could fly. A Cessna is the air force's lightest aircraft, and piloting it is incomparably easier than flying any of the fighter jets.

And so, in my condition, with my cane and my arm that won't straighten out, I convince the air force that, in the course of my studies at Bar-Ilan University, I can also be a Cessna pilot at the Sde Dov airport and perform assignments on days when I am free. I am in this marvelous state of being wherein the word "no" is simply not a part of my air force vocabulary. I do a few refresher flights before I am ready for the flight test, which is conducted by Dr. Benny Kellner, who is a pilot and the air force's medical officer. Kellner wants to gauge my functioning as a pilot. After an hour-long test flight, he authorizes me to be an active service pilot on the Cessna. The date is August 2—eight months to the day since I crossed the Suez Canal on that small ship, all encased in plaster.

I drive from Sde Dov back to Bar-Ilan, for my Intro to Economics course. Deep down I know that I'm just kidding myself and everyone else. I will not perform any missions as a Cessna pilot. That's not me, that's not my personality, that's not what I'm looking for. The fact that I can take an airplane, lift it into the air, fly it to its destination and land it, makes no impression on me. For someone who has never flown a plane it may be a great marvel. It does nothing for me. For me, flying means something else. It serves another, more serious, purpose.

I see Motti Hod, the air force commander, at one of those squadron parties that are still being held even during the War of Attrition. Of course he inquires about how I'm doing. I tell him that Dr. Kellner has approved me to be a Cessna pilot.

"Terrific," he says. "You can combine that with your studies. You'll be able to return to the world of flying, you can fly air cargo missions to the Refidim base, to the Baluza airfield, to Sharm el-Sheikh. I'm very pleased to hear about this."

I try to picture myself ferrying cargo to these bases in Sinai.

"Motti," I say, "I'm not going to do it."

His expression darkens. "Why?"

"I'm not a Cessna pilot. I fly a Cessna when I need to get someplace. I'm not going to fly missions in a Cessna."

Motti wraps his arm around my shoulder and leads me over to a far corner of the room. "Giora, I understand you, I do. But go ahead and fly in the cargo division. Work your way up in the cargo division. We plan to really develop it. You know that you'll go as far as you want to go with these planes, too."

I don't want to continue the conversation. "Forget it. I want to concentrate on my studies. And I have to get rid of this cane. I still need another little operation on my leg. I'll come to talk to you about it another time."

Motti pats me on the back. "Whenever you like, Giora."

We return to the general hubbub, to where all the pilots are standing with their pretty wives or girlfriends. Not everyone is here, though. Shmuel Hetz isn't standing here, Yitzhak Pir isn't standing here, or Menachem Eini, or Yigal Shochat or Moshe Goldwasser. They've all been killed or fallen prisoner in Egypt in the last weeks. Young Goldwasser, whose picture when he was still alive was published in the Egyptian newspapers, had been taken to a military compound, perhaps even the same prison where I was held, and there he was apparently beaten to death, maybe at the hands of my very own Sudanese giant. He returned to Israel in a coffin. The party is being held in an air force in which cracks are steadily forming, yet most people prefer to avert their eyes, to ignore it and pretend that everything is under control.

Thirty-One

27-JAN-1971

Ever since I started to think about flying, I'd been aware that there were other flight sections in the air force aside from combat. Try as I might, I just couldn't picture myself fitting in to any one of them. As a relatively young pilot at the time, I was quite ignorant of what they actually did, but the key factor for me then wasn't just what they did but how they did it. The way I saw it, military aviation came down to the ability to fly completely unfettered from the surface of the earth, in three dimensions, straight and upside down, with sharp accelerations and decelerations, at speeds that are unmatched on the ground and in planes that have no civilian counterparts.

Flying military cargo planes requires very skilled piloting. Essentially, it is the basis for civilian heavy aviation the world over. There is a lot of pride involved when a pilot attains the professional level that enables him to fly international flights, even in poor weather conditions, far from his ground control center. But flying as a purely professional pursuit just never interested me. For me, aviation was always a tool to command others, to lead people of the highest caliber, to execute military missions that could not be accomplished any other way. In those days, I saw the possibility for this in combat alone and nowhere else.

And so, the more I think it over, I just can't abide the idea of sitting in the cockpit of a cargo plane with another three crewmen beside me, and watching through the large windshield as a formation of four Mirages or Phantoms passes by, pulls upward and disappears into the deep blue in under a minute. I know that my place is in that formation and not in any other aircraft. I make my way home and, like every other night, hobble to bed with my cane, wondering if it will be a quiet night or whether I will again find myself being chased in a dream.

When the summer course at the university is over I go to see my doctor from the first day of my return to Israel, Yoel Engel. I tell him that I want him to straighten out my left arm. Yoel says, "No. Your left hand has almost complete closure, which means that you can button your shirt, you can shave, you can eat at a table normally—in short, most of the uses of your hand have been restored."

"And what about retracting the wheels after takeoff?" I ask. Yoel looks at me as if I'm mixing two completely unrelated conversations.

"In every plane, the handle is located on the front left side of the cockpit," I explain to him. "If you don't straighten out my arm, I won't be able to retract the wheels after takeoff."

Yoel has a sarcastic streak and he could easily be dismissive, but instead he plunges into a serious and in-depth explanation about the elbow—a particularly sensitive and difficult joint on which to operate, with the odds of success being even more difficult to predict.

"It could end up in an even worse state than now," he concludes.

"Yoel," I tell him, "with the genes I got from my mother, and with what you learned in Paris, my arm will be okay. Just do the surgery." And so, not long afterwards I am once again on the operating table, under full anesthesia.

The elbow is truly a stubborn joint. After the initial complex operation, to get the elbow to be able to flex as fully as possible, another person has to repeatedly bend and straighten my arm. The pain is so excruciating that this can only be done when I am under full anesthesia. Then in the afternoons I must continue with other painful physical therapy exercises. I don't want to even recall those two weeks I spent in the hospital. But when I'm finally finished with all the physical therapy, I have an arm that is only forty-five degrees shy of full straightening.

I'm a fairly tall guy, six-foot one, and at the time of my capture I weighed about 180 pounds. By the time I returned from Egypt, I'd lost about forty-five pounds, the combined result of limited, poor nutrition and shriveled muscles. My right leg is now two inches shorter than my left leg, and the military shoemakers try to offer solutions by crafting special shoes for me. My leg muscles are getting stronger, my weight has started to resemble what it used to be pre-captivity, my left arm is no longer sticking out as if waiting for someone to hang a lady's purse on the end of it. Physically, things are definitely improving.

Just two things are still bothering me—the dreams that won't go away and another internal conundrum. *Do I really want to go back to flying combat missions in the crazy region known as the Middle East?* I don't know if I even have the tools to really delve into this question. Perhaps the "cure" I found for the returning dreams is worse than the illness itself.

One of the "helpful tips" the psychologists had left me with was that the odds of a former POW being hit again are greater than the odds for a regular pilot. Evidently because of the likelihood that the performance level of someone who's been through captivity will decline in high-pressure moments. He'll avoid risk and that avoidance could compromise the mission.

What the hell am I to do?

A little more than a year after my return to Israel I decide to pay a visit to the 101st Squadron. My friend Yitzhak Nir greets me.

"Come with me," I say to him. We walk to one of the squadron's underground hangars. With Nir following behind, I walk up to a plane that's not in use.

"I want to sit in the plane," I say. He attaches the cockpit ladder to the plane, opens the canopy for me and gets out of the way. I climb up in stages, at first just peeking into the cockpit, and then continuing, entering somewhat clumsily on account of my unbending leg, and sitting down. Nir climbs up the ladder after me and stands silently looking on. I sit inside there for about ten minutes, getting reacquainted with the Mirage cockpit—the workspace for fewer than one hundred people in the entire country—and seeing what has changed due to the limitations my body has imposed on me.

I can do everything. I move the stick around. I push the throttle all the way to full afterburner and pull it back to idle. I touch (caress) the switches that activate the plane's various systems that I know so well. I bring both hands up to the upper ejection handle. Yes, I would have to release the shoulder straps for a moment in order to reach with my crippled arm to the front left corner of the cockpit, but there is no switch there that couldn't tolerate this brief pause.

"What are you planning to do?" Nir asks.

"Yitzhak," I say, "believe it or not, I'm going to fly a Mirage."

"You're crazy," he tells me, and then we walk back to the squadron building.

On Friday, January 27, 1971, thirteen and a half months after my return from captivity, I take off from the 101st Squadron for a solo flight in a Mirage. Two days before, I'd flown a two-seater Mirage at Ramat David Airbase with Uri Even-Nir, the commander of the Mirage squadron there, so he could judge if my piloting was safe.

Now I am alone, in the skies over Hatzor Airbase.

———

The air force flight school was legendary among Israeli youth. All over the country, in the big cities and small towns, in the kibbutzim and rural villages, you could meet intelligent, talented and ambitious men whose personal histories included a temporary stint in the pilots' course. In fact, barely one in ten completed the course and got to have the cloth wings pinned to the left side of his chest. Everyone who entered flight school knew from day one that the odds were stacked against him. I never believed that I'd make it and become a fighter pilot.

Only eight years before, I was seventeen, straight out of military boarding school, and on the day the course began, I was just one in a long line of one hundred and fifty cadets. The outstanding and highly competitive high school graduates were ready to make every effort to be selected into Israel's number-one volunteer unit.

Two years later, there were only fourteen graduates of Pilot Course 43.

My hands shook the first time I touched the dearly coveted wings that the air force commander pinned on my shirt. Only ten of us were assigned to fly fighter jets, and thus I set out on the path to flying single-seater aircraft, planes in which your first flight is a solo flight. At first I flew the French Ouregan and soon after I became part of a squadron that flew the Super Mystere—the first Israeli Air Force interceptor plane with an afterburner.

A year and a half after getting our wings, Ilan Gonen and I were promoted to a squadron that flew the renowned Mirage aircraft, planes that were usually only flown by much older and more experienced pilots. In the summer of 1965, on the day of my first solo flight in that rocket-like plane, I again recalled that image of the one hundred and fifty young men who began the course with me. Then I was all of twenty years and three months old, and attached to my shirt below the pilot's wings was the small skull-like symbol of the Mirage squadron from Hatzor Airbase.

"What more could a person ask for?" I thought, and at that moment I knew that the answer was—not a thing.

There is no way to truly describe the flying experience. First of all, it's the experience of a lone individual. You climb the ladder to the cockpit, put your right leg on the seat and then your left leg, gently slide into a sitting position and start to strap yourself to the seat, to the plane really, with the help of the ground crew. He hands you your crash helmet, helps you get hooked up to the oxygen system and the communications system, removes the safety catches from the ejection seat, and when he climbs down and takes the ladder with him, you close the transparent canopy. Now you're inside and the rest of the world is outside. From here on, the experience is yours alone and hard to share with others.

How to convey the feeling of the first take-off in a new plane or of gliding over a silvery cloud layer as it reflects the light of a full moon upward? And it is quite impossible to describe how it really feels to be flying at almost the speed of sound at an altitude of two hundred feet and abruptly bring your plane into a vertical position facing up into the endless sky, while lying on your back in your seat you watch the horizon slipping downward and out of sight, pulling the whole earth with it.

How can you explain what it's like when your heart skips a beat at the sight of the "fire in the engine" light illuminating, or what happens to your breathing as the sweat drips from you when you realize you've lost your spatial orientation in the pitch dark night, far away and alone above the sea? How can you ever convey the sensation of the supreme effort that is crammed into brief minutes whenever you do battle with your squadron comrades in an aerial combat drill, knowing that in a real war it will be all the harder?

This may be why so few books have been written about aerial combat, compared to other forms of warfare, and perhaps also why over time pilots tend to become taciturn techno-geeks who don't often make their presence felt at poetry readings and the like.

I was the youngest pilot to ever fly a Mirage. And it wasn't long before I started to believe that if I wasn't king of the sky, I was at least one of its princes.

Thirty-Two

1971 - 1972

A POW's parents are a whole world unto themselves. My parents, who immigrated to Mandatory Palestine in the 1920s as young Zionists, had lived through some tough years during my time in the military. They never discouraged me or showed any worry. If any worry was ever expressed, it was always in regard to the nation and the Jewish people.

Throughout my stay in Egypt, they adamantly refused to try to circumvent the air force in any way, and avoided all contact with the media, which relentlessly courted them and Miriam. They chose to go on with their daily lives without giving anyone the feeling that they were deserving of any type of special treatment. When relatives in France offered to try to obtain the assistance of Michel Debré, the former prime minister, to whom they had access, my parents firmly turned them down.

"The State of Israel and no one else will take care of Giora," was the response they repeated over and over. That, after all, was what they had left Poland for—my father at nineteen and my mother at sixteen. We never spoke about it, but in my heart I thanked them every day for having honored me so with their noble conduct.

Nonetheless, I had no idea if, by returning to flying, I was pushing them into an unbearable position. Miriam, carrying the six-month belly of her first pregnancy, had been fully aware lately that I was flying again and did not try to stop me. For her I was "invincible." She felt I was endowed with a superhuman invulnerability. Moreover, like me, she believed that flying was a crucial part of my path to getting back to being the Giora I was before September 11, 1969.

But my parents didn't know a thing, and it was important to me to hear what they had to say when I informed them about this. My return to flying had many unspoken implications. I knew that I was placing quite a burden on them, but I knew that in the tradition of refraining from outward displays of emotion—which was essentially the platform upon which my mother and father had conducted their parallel lives of building a state and building a family—they would keep their inner turmoil to themselves.

Towards evening I called to speak with my father.

"This morning I flew a Mirage," I told him.

His answer was not long in coming. "I congratulate you." And then he was silent.

Knowing what an emotional person he was beneath his formal façade, I revived the conversation. I told him a little about the flight and promised that on Friday night, at the Sabbath meal, we'd find the time to talk so I could tell him about my plans.

"I congratulate you," my father said again. And I knew that he was sitting at home in his armchair, with tears welling up in his eyes.

In all the world, there is no lower place to which one can fall than the cold concrete floor of solitary confinement. And on all the planet there is no place more remote than an enemy prison cell in wartime. In Egypt I did not yet fully appreciate how vital it was that I resume flying, not just flying but combat aviation in fighter jets. This was the only way for me to reclaim my old life.

In Egypt, in solitary confinement, I had made up my mind that I would fly again, if only just because I had said so to Sayeed in the heat of a moment when I was struggling to retain my dignity and independence, to preserve my masculinity. A fairly childish reason to go and get yourself strapped into a plane that often flies at twice the speed of sound at altitudes at which the skies above start to take on a black hue. But now, here in Israel, having passed the "technical" stage—yes, I am capable of flying a Mirage—I had to embark on the more difficult quest, much harder than captivity itself—the quest to erase all traces of captivity from the psyche.

The solo flight I made thirteen months after my return from Egypt signaled to me that I now possessed the technical tools I needed in order to get my previous life back. I was one of the hundred or so people in Israel who could get into the cockpit of a Mirage and fly the plane. Now I had to decide if I had the strength to embark on the brutal journey (far rougher than I even suspected at the time) to expunge captivity from my being and get back to being just like anyone else.

One day in the summer of 1971, I informed Iftach Spector, the commander of the Mirage squadron that I'd been a part of for the last six months, that I could advance from being a pilot who only flew training flights to an operational pilot who took part in the squadron's flight missions. It was a decision I'd reached through the sort of dialogue one conducts solely with himself.

Ever since I resumed flying in the Mirage, I'd been careful not to consult with anyone about any move I made. I didn't think I could expect anyone in the air force to have an objective discussion with me about the thorny question of a disabled ex-POW pilot who wants to fly again. Certainly not one who wants to fly operational missions. Most amazing of all was that not a single commander, of any rank, made any effort to delve into that dark world.

So Giora's flying? He's not causing any trouble? He's not asking for any help? Terrific! Now come on, let's go to the officers' mess and have lunch!

My commanders' avoidance of talking about the subject with me almost surely derived from the meager emotional skills that were typical of commanders in that era. Perhaps the paucity or absence of such skills is an inevitable part of the military commander's personality profile. Thus he can withstand the pressures that characterize military life in general and combat in particular. Perhaps it can be attributed to the Spartan upbringing most of them received in the 1940s and 1950s, or to an ideology that exalted the collective far above the individual. Or perhaps just because we all are reluctant to probe things that seem akin to entering a dark cave teeming with scorpions, a black hole that might one day pull us in too. Although we'd prefer to believe that if something like that should happen to us, we won't have any trouble emerging from it unscathed: Just look at Giora.

I'm not too sure that, years later when my contemporaries and I attained the highest command ranks, we were any different, but our subordinates will have to be the judge of that. In any event, not only wasn't there a single person in the air force who tried to talk with me about all of this, there wasn't anyone to whom I could turn of my own initiative. No one to consult with, not to mention anyone to lean on for assistance.

Nor did I want to. All decisions as to how to make my way back into the regular air force frameworks were to be left to me exclusively. I'd completed six months of training flights and was feeling very good in the airplane. *Come on*, I said to myself, *let's try to move up another rung on the ladder that leads to where the best of the best are found.*

Spector didn't express any reservations and suggested that I come be his number two for a weekend of intercept alert duty at the Refidim air base in the Sinai desert. And so one Friday afternoon I decided to take an airplane and go down to Refidim to replace Spector's partner and spend the weekend there.

It was nearly two years since the last time I landed at the base. I organized all my personal gear, then went over to my intercept alert plane and examined it. I adjusted the length of the ejection seat straps, connected the helmet to the radio and placed it in the usual spot, by the head of the ejection seat, ready for the ground crew to hand it to the pilot the moment he is belted in to take off for the intercept mission.

An "intercept mission" is a mission to defend the country's skies against infiltration by unwanted aircraft. In many countries, this is a routine assignment generally confined to dealing with planes that have mistakenly strayed from their intended flight path. In countries that are in a state of war, or military tension at least, such a mission involves intercepting planes that penetrate your airspace with hostile intent, whether on a reconnaissance mission or an actual assault. This is the fighter pilot's top mission.

This was the first time I had been so close to Egypt since I resumed flying. I sat in the intercept alert room, started to leaf through the various newspapers, and discovered that I couldn't read. Restless, I paced the room and the airplane lot, unable to shake the idea that a ring of the bell would have me over the Suez Canal within seven minutes.

My nervousness kept growing. I counted the minutes that still had to pass until the last light of day, when we would shed our flight suits and be free for the night... until first light. The atmosphere in the "villa," as the intercept alert building was called, was just as I'd always remembered it. The dinner preparations, the not-too-surprising surprise at finding a 16-mm projector there which meant that we could watch *To Sir with Love* with Sidney Poitier for the umpteenth time, the local gossip about the air force and about what happened to whom, a few games of dominoes, and shortly after that, trying to sleep.

Soon I found myself lying in bed, under the disgusting air force-issue wool blanket, unable to nod off. I turned from side to side, I shifted positions, I turned the light on and then off again, but all to no avail. Or maybe I did sleep but I felt like I was awake. At long last, sunrise came to my rescue and I could happily get up, go outside to check over the plane and test the communications with the base's control tower and then go back inside. I didn't go back to sleep, as we normally used to do. Instead, I sat in the lounge doing crossword puzzles, reading and trying to get a handle on my uneasiness. That Saturday felt much like the day before, like both the day and night that is. A quiet tension crawling below the skin like a column of ants, difficulty remaining engaged in any sort of activity, and a mouth that was unusually dry and in constant need of water.

When I took off on Sunday to return to Hatzor, it was after nearly thirty-six hours with no sleep, either during the night between Friday and Saturday, or the night between Saturday and Sunday. I was relieved to get away from the Egyptian border. I realized now that captivity was still haunting me, and that the fears it planted in me were going to be harder to rein in than I'd thought.

I went to Jaffa to meet with the air force attorney. I wanted to find out what would happen if I ever became a POW again. Attorneys are good people, but when you walk out of a meeting with them, you are left facing a dilemma. The attorney said that such a situation was not directly addressed in the Geneva Convention, but since I'd been returned in a prisoner exchange—i.e., the goodwill of the nation that freed me was part of the process, that nation would have reason to expect that I not return there to fight again. He said that if I were captured again, they might claim that I was not protected by the Geneva Convention. He couldn't tell me if this was the accepted interpretation in other countries, too.

When I walked out of the beautiful, Arabesque-style house in Jaffa where the air force attorney's office was located, I knew in my gut that if I should ever meet Sayeed or Aziz again, not to mention the Sudanese giant, they wouldn't be seeking any consultations with their attorney on how to deal with me.

And so, before I knew it, I was back to being an operational pilot in the 101st Mirage Squadron. During the week I was a student at Bar-Ilan University. On Fridays I flew training flights. And every now and again I was one of the two pilots on intercept alert in the squadron building, waiting for the ringing of the bell or the wail of the siren, which Anwar had been so keen to know about.

The dreams were appearing less often now, maybe once a week at most, and I assumed that their frequency would continue to decline. I'd learned to wake myself, to lie absolutely still and calm down, and then go back to sleep. I'd also learned to live with my physical limitations—my short right leg that bent at the knee no more than eighty degrees, and my left arm that wouldn't straighten out. I got used to going down to Refidim for intercept alert duty once in a while, though I never forgot for a moment that I was different than the other three pilots in the room. Brigadier General Yehezkel Somekh, the deputy air force commander, summoned me for an interview and tried to convince me to halt my university studies and to take an active role again in one of the squadrons. But I stuck to my original plan: earn my degree, do a moderate amount of flying and continue with my medical upgrades.

During one of the trimester breaks I was once again lying on Henri Horoshovsky and Yoel Engel's operating table. It was the sixth operation since my return, and this routine of classes, exams, an operation at Tel Hashomer during the break, then back to class and so on, seemed perfectly normal to me, as if it were an ordinary schedule for most people. Coming around from the anesthesia in the recovery room with that feeling of thirst and hazy consciousness, the pain in the days following the incision in the flesh, the complications, the occasional inflammation as a result of infection, and the return yet again to the world of the hospital—to me all this was the price that had to be paid in order to check off the box entitled "Attempt to Erase as Many Lingering Effects of Captivity as Possible."

This time, Yoel removed the seventeen-inch stainless steel nail from my thigh, around which my new thigh bone had been reconstructed. And while I was still lying in the recovery room, he went out and presented it to Miriam, who was sitting in the waiting room.

Miriam is one of those women who never throw anything away. And I mean anything. She gave the nail to artist Igael Tumarkin, along with the screw that the Egyptians had inserted in my elbow and which she had also kept since it was removed, and at his request, added some more items related to my past. When I came home a week later, Tumarkin's collage, an incredibly beautiful piece of work, was waiting for me.

In the summer of 1972 I finished my degree, was promoted to the rank of major and appointed deputy commander of the 113th Squadron, an Ouragan squadron whose main job was to train the latest graduates of the pilots' course. All of my fellow graduates from Pilot Course 43 had already been promoted to major four months earlier. To my complete stupefaction, I'd been told that the promotion applied to everyone except me. The reason: Everyone else had been performing the duties of a major while I was "living it up" at university. I went to speak with Rafi Harlev, the commander of Hatzor Air Force Base at the time.

"Rafi," I said to him, "On March 12, Giora Kenin, Benrom, Elisha and all the rest of my comrades are being promoted to major. Why not me? Especially since I attained the rank of captain nearly a year before them after I was the top flying ace in the Six Day War?"

"Because you're a student," Rafi said to me. "And students are not promoted in the course of their studies."

"But you know that the circumstances that led me to go to university at this point in my life weren't exactly business as usual around here. You know as well as anyone that I'd give anything for my life's trajectory to have turned out differently—so that right now I'd be in the Phantom squadron and not at university." All of my attempts to plead my special situation came to naught. For my commanders, in the spirit of "enough with all the personal circumstances" that may have characterized the air force at the time, the refusal was absolute and final. I was left at the rank of captain, having been given yet another lesson on the air force's outlook that, as far as it was concerned, there was nothing out of the ordinary about me. When I told the story to air force commander Motti Hod a few months later, he listened attentively, and since by then I was nearly finished with my university exams, he wanted to make it up to me and insisted on personally conferring upon me the rank of major, just as he had attached the captain's insignia to my sleeve at the air force victory party in Jerusalem right after the Six Day War. I went to meet him at the Sde Dov airport, where he was holding some meeting, and there I was promoted to major, more than five years after I achieved the rank of captain.

Returning to a full-time command role shot me full of energy and gave me a new zest for life. In addition to my intense activity as deputy commander of the squadron that trained the newly minted flight school graduates, I was put in charge of the squadron's preparations to take on the new Nesher planes. These were French Mirages that were partially manufactured in Israel and fully assembled here and which were slated to take the place of the Ouragans when those were taken out of service. It was a marvelous time. I flew nonstop and I was working with the young pilot course graduates, a new group every four months, impressive fellows who would obviously go far. I was flying both types of aircraft, and I was busy writing up all the necessary literature so that we could be an operational intercept squadron as soon as the Ouragans were replaced with the Neshers. I was back to being part of the older and more experienced group of pilots at Hatzor Airbase.

My daughter Netta, now a year and a half old, was an important anchor in my daily life, and I eagerly awaited the day when I could read to her at bedtime from *Winnie the Pooh*, the book that was with me in captivity and had been an island of optimism in that sea of suffering and dwindling hope.

Everything was taking on new life, and the not-so-distant past seemed virtually forgotten.

Inside, I knew it wasn't so. From time to time I would go out on intercept patrol in the north when the air force was conducting some type of operation in Syria or Lebanon. There was nothing special about these patrols. The route ran from the northern tip of the Sea of Galilee to the city of Kiryat Shmona just south of the Lebanon border, and resembled an elongated numeral eight because of the turns made at each end. The left turn at the northernmost point always looped around Kiryat Shmona and briefly sent the formation into Lebanese territory. It was a tiny swing across the border, just a couple of miles perhaps. I knew that to all the other pilots in the formation, the Lebanon section of the flight meant nothing. Like countless times before, they were sitting in the cockpits of their planes, banking forty-five degrees to the left in order to execute the turn, gazing down and to the left and scanning—with some boredom—the mountainous terrain dotted with villages that kept disappearing beneath the nose of the aircraft. And the whole time they were waiting for the operation to conclude with the call over the radio: "Alright, let's go home," or else for the formation to be called upon for a significant mission.

But meanwhile I just grew increasingly tense and nervous whenever we were across the border. Flying over enemy territory, even if it was only Lebanon, to which no one gave much thought at the time, caused me much distress. No matter how many times I told myself that it was ridiculous, that it was stupid, and that even if I were to parachute from the plane, the western wind would invariably carry me into Israel, logic always surrendered each time anew to the physical sensations that accompanied that when-will-this-end-already feeling. When will we cross the border again back into Israel?

I wanted to think that I was immersed in a kind of strenuous self-training effort, and that the more times I made the trip, the easier and more ordinary it would become, and then I could be just like all the other pilots again. But that didn't happen. And the very intimate inner knowledge that my captivity had permeated not only my physical being but my consciousness as well, kept coming back to me in private moments, in moments when I tried to imagine what would happen when it wasn't just a quick jut into Lebanon but a much deeper penetration into enemy territory.

Thirty-Three

9-Nov-1972

There are four of us in the briefing—Avi Lanir, the leader of the formation, Ilan Gonen, Yaakov Gal and me. It is a short and relatively simple briefing. We're going out on patrol over the Golan Heights because of suspicious and intensive activity by the Syrian Air Force there since midday. I will be Avi Lanir's partner. Gal and Gonen will be the other pair. Nothing unusual here, and we all head off to take care of any last arrangements before boarding the planes.

An hour later, we're over the central Golan Heights, patrolling north and south. Fifteen minutes pass and then the intercept controller reports on a Syrian formation patrolling directly parallel to us, to the east. I start to think about the four Syrian planes that are essentially a mirror image of our formation. Is there someone in Syria like Anwar? And if so, is he sitting in a MiG-21 right now thirty miles to the east of me?

"I'm taking you into battle," says the controller, yanking me out of the brief reverie in which my thoughts had strayed back in time to Anwar. The tension is mounting but he keeps us on the patrol route for two minutes longer, before directing us northeast "to the engagement."

To the engagement—the phrase that sends a high-voltage current rippling through the intercept pilot's entire being. The phrase that means within moments you will find yourself in the midst of an action that may well culminate with some of the participants killed, others still alive but forced to parachute from their planes, and the rest returning home to land. Everything happens very fast.

We turn east and accelerate, the Syrians turn west toward us, and the distance between us rapidly shrinks as we close upon one another at approximately twice the speed of sound. When we jettison the two reserve fuel tanks, I know that I am heading into my first dogfight since the one in which I was hit, exactly three years ago. At the closing speed at which we are approaching one another, the Syrians and us, the distance is reduced by about five hundred yards per second. My rear end is still reverberating from the jolt to both wings from the dumping of the fuel tanks when we spot them directly ahead of us. There are four of them.

Their left pair, painted in the Syrians' brown-and-green camouflage colors, passes very close to Lanir and me on the left. Lanir immediately pulls up high and left. I roll over on my back and "dig" deep left, aiming to exploit the ability to maintain my speed in this way to do a better turn ratio and, after executing a full three hundred and sixty-degree turn, arrive behind the enemy planes, at the "advantage position." As I pull up from below, out of the corner of my left eye I can see the two MiGs, still flying together about a half-mile ahead of me, making a sharp eastward turn, and out of the corner of my right eye I see Lanir completing his high turn and descending, so that the two of us are now converging toward a point where we will almost certainly collide. I slow the rate of my turn slightly, Lanir enters the imaginary meeting point before me, and when we are both facing north, he fires a missile.

One of the MiGs is hit and explodes.

While the missile was making its way through the air, I cut in front of Lanir from the left so I am now the forward plane, homing in on the second MiG. The whole dogfight is like a carousel spinning very quickly to the left, with the four of us—now just the three of us—on the edges of the giant disk and trying to catch up to the rider ahead of us. The MiG continues in its tight left turn and when it comes to be facing west it enters the glare of the enormous sun now sinking low over the horizon and vanishes. I continue my turn, as I wait for the MiG to emerge from the sun's glare from the south, but I don't see it.

I hear Ilan Gonen reporting that he downed a MiG to the north of us, and this is immediately followed by the controller's instruction, "Cease battle."

My MiG reappears to the southeast, and I need only to cover very little space to achieve firing position. Lanir reports that he can see Gal and Gonen, and that they are all joining up. I see the MiG turn over on its back and dive toward the ground, getting swallowed up by the shadows covering the dark earth of the Golan Heights. I roll over and lower my nose to dive after him. On the radio I hear Lanir reporting that they are on their way to Quneitra, the small Syrian town in the Golan Heights on the border between Israel and Syria, asking where I am and urging me to drop everything and join them. I have no choice. I must abandon eye contact with the MiG, give up the chance to shoot it down, head back westward and join the other three. I start to pull up the nose to come out of the dive, and I let the MiG go.

As I am crossing the horizon, heading east at a very high speed that is taking me deeper into Syria at the rate of about 300 yards per second, to my left on the ground I see the Syrian town of Al-Sanamayn and to my right on the ground the town of Jassem. All of a sudden, without warning, fear grips me in its most aggressive form. The three other planes in my formation are already on their way to Quneitra, the MiG I was chasing has surely descended by now to a very low altitude, out of my reach, and meanwhile I've fallen into a trap where I am stuck at 20,000 feet, between the Golan Heights and Damascus, smack in the sights of the Syrian surface-to-air missile batteries.

I turn west to head home, knowing I am giving up the opportunity to spot missiles coming from the east, from my rear sector. My legs start to shake inside the cockpit, and I can't get the shaking to stop or even think too much about it because my mind is feverishly seeking an answer to the question of how to get out the hell out of here. I point the nose down to dive to a lower altitude, but then the not so clever thought hits me that this is actually the anti-aircraft fire zone and if I go too low I might get hit. I raise the nose again and break sharply ninety degrees right and left to dodge any missiles that might be heading my way. I am still well within reach of the Syrian missile batteries, which must surely be trying to lock in on me, identify me as a hostile target and shoot me down. I realize, though, that if I continue flying this way, with all these breaking and clearing turns, I will never reach my destination to the west.

The perspiration, the rapid breathing, the leg tremors—it's all swirling together when Lanir comes over the radio, asking what's up with me. Faithful to the behavioral code of Israeli pilots in combat, I muster my last bits of energy to answer calmly in a tone that says, "Don't worry, everything's under control," that I am on my way out.

What comes next are five minutes of flying packed with evasive maneuvers, with my head swiveling from side to side in the cockpit as I strain to get a maximal view of what's happening behind me, and my breathing coming hard and fast like a sprinter. Five of the longest minutes of my life until at last I see Quneitra, and throughout that five minutes I'm not at all sure I won't come apart at the seams before I make it back across the border into Israel. Quneitra is below me now, and I can turn left and head southward, as I gaze toward the Syrian missile array from which I just escaped.

The leg tremors haven't stopped, I feel a cold shiver up my spine and I can tell that my flight suit is totally soaked with sweat. I flip the oxygen switch to the 100-percent setting, both to give my lungs more fuel and just to see if I can still use my hands, which for the last five crazy minutes have been squeezing the life out of the stick and the throttle. Lanir says they are above the village of Yavne'el in the Galilee and asks if they should wait for me.

"I'll come back alone," I reply, knowing I will need plenty of time to pull myself together. It's evening now, and I climb to 25,000 feet and slow the plane's speed so the trip will take a bit longer. My breathing gradually returns to normal, my legs stop shaking and all that's left is the discomfort of the drenched flight suit. I look down and behold a dearly cherished sight. The sight of my small country slowly passing underneath me at the speed of the flight, lights coming on as it shifts at its own pace from day to night. A small country that surely hasn't the slightest idea of what is happening above it in the skies. No one knows, and the mixture of terror and shame churns my stomach.

Thirty-Four

12-Nov-1972

After landing at Hatzor and going through the combat debriefing, I arrive home at eight in the evening. I lie down on the bed, still in the flight suit, and sleep until morning, completely cut off from the world. The next day is a Friday, the start of the weekend. On Saturday night, after forty-eight hours of agonizing, I know that this was apparently my last flight. It just isn't something a human being can cope with. Being in air combat after you've been in captivity requires a mental toughness that I evidently lack. The time has come to do something about it.

On Sunday morning I inform the squadron that I won't be coming to fly and I go to see Rafi Harlev, the wing commander. Rafi is one of those people who know how to listen, and he also spares you all the psychological analyses that commanders are often fond of indulging in.

All he says is, "I want you to go tell this to Motti."

His secretary gets Motti Hod, the air force commander, on the phone. "Motti, Giora Romm is sitting here with me. I want you meet him and have a talk with him." A brief pause, and then Rafi again, "No, not later this week. Today." Another pause, and then, "Sir, I'm telling you it must be today. I'm asking you to find time *today*."

Thirty seconds later, Rafi turns to me and says, "The air force commander will see you in his office at four." In the air force, people refer to each other by first names. When someone is referred to by his official title, it's a code that means the speaker feels this is a serious matter.

At four o'clock I am sitting across from Motti in his office. I tell him all about what happened to me. Now Rafi is a very good listener, but Motti even surpasses him. There are no extraneous distractions, he doesn't say much yet you clearly feel that he is with you. When I finish recounting my experience, I fall silent and fix my eyes on him.

"Giora," says Motti, "I can't give you any advice. We don't have anyone in the air force who has been through what you've been through and what you're going through. I can't think and decide for you. But I am the air force commander and I'm telling you that whatever you decide, I will personally see to it that it happens. You can go off tomorrow and become a pilot for El Al, you can go back to university, you can choose a military career path that's unrelated to flying and you can decide anything else you like. Whatever you decide, I and the entire air force will be behind you."

I don't fly the next day either. The internal cracks are refusing to mend. I can't talk with anyone. Not even Miriam. The incident has shaken me with a force like nothing I've ever felt before. In all my operational experience up to now, even in situations where the environment was especially hostile, I never felt as threatened and helpless as I did in that last dogfight. I know without a doubt that it is a consequence of captivity, but I struggle to rationally put a label on the problem I am up against.

Ron Ronen calls to congratulate me for having participated in a dogfight again for the first time. Others do the same. Everyone thinks I'm a hero. But inside me those feelings of near-mental breakdown from captivity have resurfaced full force, that terrible feeling when you just want to explode but don't know how or when.

When afternoon comes, I phone the squadron and request to have an Ouragan plane ready for me by twilight, for regular flight. As evening approaches, when the base is quiet and most people are leaving for home, and the skies are clear of other planes, I take off. I take the plane to the Kfar Menachem area. The train tracks to Be'er Sheva pass near the village and there is a section that is straight as a ruler, a section that is perfect for performing aerobatics.

I start doing aerobatics along the path of the train tracks. Nothing too extreme. Nothing strenuous. Just lazy and slow aerobatics that mesh with the total silence surrounding the plane. In aerobatics, every time, no matter what maneuver you are performing, the plane's nose crosses the horizon as it heads upward, forging its path with nothing but sky visible and meeting the horizon on the other side when the plane is on its back, and then "plows" the bottom of the imaginary sphere in which it is maneuvering.

My eyes take in a wide range of items on the ground—the train tracks, a plowing tractor, the houses of Kfar Menachem on the right, someone burning a pile of dry wood, and again the horizon appears, now directly opposite, then on the right, then on the left. And sometimes all it takes is a slow roll around the plane's horizontal axis to give you that blissful feeling...

what on the ground could ever compare to this magic of flying? What could ever compensate for the feeling of loss if I gave it up?

With five hundred liters of fuel remaining, I turn back to take the plane in for a landing, and on the way from Kfar Menachem to Hatzor, I know for a fact that I don't have the emotional strength to do the right thing—to give in and stop flying.

Thirty-Five

6-OCT-1973

It's 3:00 p.m. on a Saturday when I line up on Runway 33 at Tel Nof. I am Yachin Kochava's number two, and our target is the Budapest outpost at the northern tip of the Suez Canal, toward Port Said. I am sitting in a Skyhawk plane loaded with eight quarter-ton bombs, and when I look to my left I see Uri Bina and Roni Tepper also lining up on the runway to complete the formation. There is nothing remarkable about any of this except in regards to me. Although I am number two, I am the commander of the squadron, the 115th Squadron, and when I take off, it will be the first time in my life that I am flying a Skyhawk.

In the history of military aviation, only three pilots have made their first sortie in a new aircraft on an operational flight. I am about to be the fourth. Just an hour and a half ago I entered the cockpit of this completely unfamiliar plane for the first time, and now I'm about to take it up in the air, fully loaded with bombs, to attack a target in an area where battles are raging.

Three days earlier, Lieutenant Colonel Ami Goldstein (Goldy), the squadron commander, was killed in a training accident. That evening, when I returned to my home in Hatzor, I found a message that Benny Peled, the air force commander, wished to speak with me. As usual, he got right to the point: Be here tomorrow at 7:30 a.m. I'm appointing you commander of the 115th Squadron.

I drive to Tel Nof Airbase where the squadron is stationed, to see Ron Ronen, the base commander, who was the one who'd insisted that I be given the command of the 115th Squadron. I've known Ron for many years. He was my commander in the 119th Squadron during the Six Day War. He was the commander of the flight school when I was a flight instructor there for two and a half years. And most important, on September 11, 1969, he was Tulip One, the leader of the Tulip formation, when I was Tulip Four, who did not return.

"Ron" I say as soon as the meeting starts, "You may not know this but I have never flown a Skyhawk."

"I know, Giora," he replies. "But I still want you, and nobody else, as the squadron commander. We have a funeral tomorrow. Afterwards, on Thursday and Friday, you'll get acquainted with the squadron, and on Sunday, you'll start a conversion course on the plane. A week from now no one will even remember that you'd never flown it before."

"Are you sure?" I ask him.

"Giora, it wasn't easy to appoint you. There are people in the force with more seniority than you who've been waiting to obtain a squadron command, and Benny was hesitant to break the regular order. I want you! ...Come on, since you're here already, come with me to see Nechama, Goldy's wife."

"His widow, Ron, his widow."

At seven-thirty the next morning in his office, Benny Peled doesn't waste any time on sentimentalities. One commander was killed, another commander is taking his place, life goes on, end of story. We speak for about ten minutes. No mention is made of the possibility that war could erupt in a couple of days. The subject of captivity is mentioned briefly, but Benny is the only one who brings it up. He says he will tell the IDF Chief of Staff at their next work meeting that he's appointed a former POW to be commander of a combat squadron. I've never had an opportunity to tell Benny about the crises that I've been struggling to overcome ever since my return to operational flying, and the subject doesn't come up now either. I'd planned to find a time to talk to him about it, but now is certainly not that time. Nor is there any point in discussing any technical issues regarding the squadron. He and I both know that my knowledge of the Skyhawk and its operations is basically nil.

The Skyhawk is primarily a plane meant for striking ground targets, while I'm coming from years of flying intercept missions and being in aerial dogfights. It's the start of the workday. Benny has an entire air force to run and isn't free to indulge in idle chitchat (and at this point I know nothing about the growing tension with Syria and Egypt).

"Go on, go meet the pilots, take over the squadron and start commanding it. Good luck to you." And so, life's never-ending rollercoaster now leads me to yet another unexpected destination—the Skyhawk squadron building in Tel Nof.

Goldy was an especially popular and beloved commander, and the air of shock and grief is palpable. I introduce myself to all the squadron pilots who are there—a few I know from my time in the air force so far, but many are new faces to me. The deputy squadron commander shows me around the facilities, and by then it is afternoon.

A large crowd stands over Goldy's freshly dug grave in the Kiryat Shaul cemetery. I observe the people gathered at the funeral, my new role having yet to fully sink in. Anat and Nili, the squadron secretaries, lay wreaths on the grave, their eyes red from crying. The honor guard fires off three rounds, and the throng begins to disperse. Small clusters of mourners trickle past me and shake my hand, whether in congratulations or polite rebuff I can't be sure.

The next day, Friday, seems completely normal at first, but the state of alert soon begins to rise, and by nightfall, with the High Holy Day of Yom Kippur setting the mood, I decide to stay and sleep at Tel Nof, on the couch in Omri Afek's home in the family quarters.

The blare of the siren at seven in the morning essentially marks the start of the three weeks of the Yom Kippur War. It's the Six Day War in reverse. Syrian and Egypt have launched a surprise attack. We suffer major loses.

In the conference room with Ron, we are informed that at 11:30 the air force will strike the Syrian Air Force on the ground, and each commander immediately rushes to his unit. This is the order for Operation Negiha ("Ramming") and I must see to all the preparations for the 115th Squadron to smoothly carry out this order. Obviously I'm going to have to find a way as soon as possible to do a quick flight to familiarize myself with the aircraft.

In the midst of all the hubbub, I dispatch one of the pilots to my home in Hatzor to fetch my flight suit and special flight boots. Mickey Schneider, the squadron's safety officer—who six days later would fly with me on a strike mission in Syria, be hit by a surface-to-air missile and fall into a grueling eight-month captivity—goes and comes back with flight gear for me: helmet, oxygen mask, G-suit and torso harness—the piece of gear with which the pilot attaches himself to the ejection seat and parachute.

Golda Meir and Moshe Dayan decide that the strike is a mistake, so the whole "Ramming" plan is off the table. This means, at least, that I have time to instruct that one plane have all its external cargo unloaded so I can take a little flight to get acquainted with my squadron's aircraft.

Avraham Yakir, one of the youngest fellows in the squadron, escorts me to the plane and explains the main points to me. "Our Skyhawk is different than all the others. It's the most modern plane in the air force, equipped with the most advanced systems."

Everything a person would normally learn in ten days I must absorb in just fifteen minutes. Yakir helps me get hooked up to the communications system, goes over the layout of the cockpit, explains how to get strapped in, how to operate the various systems, how to start this up. And then he climbs down and takes the ladder with him. As he would tell me a few months later, not long before he was killed in a training accident, he thought all along that this whole thing was some kind of practical joke.

I start up the plane, carefully taxi over to takeoff position and run through all the necessary checks, but then I can't close the cockpit canopy. Repeated explanations are offered to me over the squadron radio, but try as I might, I can't shut the thing. A pickup truck drives up with Yakir riding in it. He mounts the wing, climbs toward the cockpit and shows me that in American planes there are certain actions—such as closing and locking the canopy—that are accomplished by sheer elbow grease, unlike in the French Mirage, where a much more delicate touch is used. Now I line up on the runway and request permission for takeoff. It's Saturday, at exactly 2:00 p.m.

"Peach, Egyptian planes are en route to attack the base. Do not take off! Return to your position immediately!"

I return the Skyhawk 410 to the position from which I took it. Yakir is waiting for me in the underground shelter where planes are kept protected from airstrikes, and he drives me back to the squadron. Pilots in full flight gear, clutching maps and aerial photos, are standing in front of the squadron building ready to go to the planes. I stop one of them and ask where he's headed.

"Our formation is going to attack Egyptian forces that are trying to take the Budapest outpost." I take the maps and photos from him.

"Who is the leader?" I ask.

"Kochava," he tells me. Yachin Kochava was my first student in the pilot training course.

"Yachin," I say to him, "as of this minute I am your number two. This is my first flight in a Skyhawk. After takeoff, it'll take about twenty minutes to reach Nahal Yam. In that time I'll learn to fly this plane, and if I have any questions, you'll answer them."

Kibbutz Nahal Yam is on the north shore of the Sinai Peninsula. In one of the long nights with Aziz, he kept prodding me to divulge the purpose of the tall antennas at Nahal Yam. In a short while, I'm going to begin the final run to the attack from these antennas, whose purpose is just as mysterious to me now as it was then. And now I am back on the runway again, already asking Kochava what the takeoff speed should be for the heavy configuration in which we are flying.

"Raise the nose at 125 knots," he tells me. "Take off at 150 and you'll be fine."

Now we're airborne and I'm still trying to orient myself in this unfamiliar cockpit, fiddling with the knobs that adjust the height of the seat and pedals, and trying to identify the multitude of buttons on the stick, which is so different from the one I'm used to in the Mirage. My eyes are busily scanning the cockpit in an effort to figure out what all the switches are, but at the same time I am pleased to see that I am exactly where I should be in the formation. It's a huge relief to see that the basic act of flying a plane is second nature for me at this point.

Over the controller's channel I hear Shlomo Levy from the 113th Squadron, the Mirage squadron, the squadron of which I was the deputy commander until just a few days ago, leading a formation on intercept patrol over the Suez Canal region. For a few seconds I can't help envying him while I contemplate my peculiar situation, thinking that where I rightfully belong is at the head of that formation instead of Shlomo. But I can't let myself get caught up in self-pity, for I must keep studying the interior of the Skyhawk cockpit, my new home in the sky.

Approaching Nahal Yam, we descend to a low altitude. With Kochava's help, I activate the ammunition switches and we accelerate toward the Budapest outpost. Kochava calls over the radio, "Pulling!" and in tandem with him, for the first time in my life, in a fully loaded Skyhawk, I pull up to execute a bombing pass the likes of which I've never tried before. At 6,000 feet we both roll over on our backs and have the outpost in sight. It's easy to spot the Egyptian amphibious armored vehicles emerging from the sea and heading for land. When we all come out of the bombing pass and join up in neat formation, Uri Bina says to me, "Two, your bombs did not release."

We're coming back up on Nahal Yam, and now I turn around to try another bombing pass, alone this time. This will be the second bombing pass I have ever attempted with the Skyhawk's advanced bombing computer, a system I'd never used until ten minutes ago. I can hardly make heads or tails out of the abundance of information contained in the image on its gunsight. This time I gently guide the sensitive aiming point on the gunsight's sophisticated Head-Up display, and when I press the button to drop the bombs I feel the plane vibrate as all eight are released.

From far to my left, from the direction of Port Said, a surface-to-air missile zooms my way. I dive until I'm practically licking the ground, and the missile loses its way and explodes in the dunes. I return to Nahal Yam, join my new companions, and we're on our way home to Tel Nof.

Kochava calls for a fuel check. Roni Tepper and Uri Bina both report 4,500 pounds. Now where can the fuel gauge in the Skyhawk be? I eventually locate it in the bottom right corner of the front panel. It reads 1,800 pounds. I realize immediately that I failed to activate the fuel transfer from the reserve tanks to the main tank.

I report 4,500. I'm not about to humiliate myself by letting it be known that I don't know how to transfer fuel. In the French-made Mirage, fuel transfer from the external fuel tanks is automatic, but these American planes must have a special switch for this somewhere. Where the hell is the switch for the fuel tanks? I can't find the bloody thing. Now the fuel gauge shows 1,600 pounds. I reach behind me with my left hand and, moving clockwise, systematically proceed to flip all the switches in the cockpit to the "on" position. At El Arish, at 20,000 feet, the needle drops to 1,400 pounds. And then, suddenly, thank god, it starts to rise. The fuel from the reserve tanks is making its way to the main tank. I make a mental note that when I'm back on the ground I'll have to see just which switch accomplished this neat trick.

"Two, one-fifty," says Kochava in the frugal language of aerial communications. And now I'm circling Tel Nof and stabilizing my plane at a speed of 150 knots on the final approach to make my first ever landing in a Skyhawk. The landing is simple. The plane's wheels caress Runway 36 the moment they touch it, and I quickly clear off the runway and taxi back to the underground shelter. I'm in a hurry. I have no time to waste. This looks like war, I have a squadron to command and I haven't had a moment yet to step back and ponder my extraordinary situation. But before I can stop to consider the implications of being thrust into this new aircraft after my experience in captivity, I have a squadron to lead in which I don't even know half the pilots, nor can I remember the technical officer's name, and when we went looking this morning for Kobi the adjutant, so he could attend to all of the urgent administrative matters, we learned that he'd skipped out the day before and gone home to Haifa.

All the squadron and unit commanders from the base assemble for a "command group" meeting with Ron late that evening. When the meeting is over, I stay behind to speak with him privately. "Ron, I know that you appointed me to command the squadron and I thank you for that, but war probably wasn't part of the game plan. If you want, find yourself a commander with experience in the Skyhawk and I'll go back to the Mirages."

For reasons I will never fathom, Ron looks at me and says, "I want you to continue. Go back to the squadron and continue as commander."

I turn on my heels, get into the car that until Wednesday belonged to Goldy, and return to that black hole—the 115th Squadron, in the Yom Kippur War.

Thirty-Six

6-OCT-1973

There is much excitement in the squadron. Everyone has returned safely from their various missions. The tumult is obscuring my attempt to make more sense of my new reality, an attempt that doesn't seem to be going very well. I feel completely out of place. For the first time in my life, I'm among a bunch of people wearing flight suits, and I don't know their names. I'm not even sure what's in each room of the squadron command building. In the operations room, one floor below ground level, several squadron officers are talking on telephones, and I have no idea whom they're talking to or what about.

I ask beautiful Nili, the operations secretary, to call all the pilots into the briefing room so I can try to put things in some order. When I enter the room, it suddenly falls silent. The middle chair in the front row is waiting empty. This is the squadron commander's seat. I walk past it, ascend the podium and, for the next half hour, try to establish an efficient framework in which we can function.

As I'm standing on the podium, speaking and giving instructions, I'm conducting a parallel dialogue with myself, on a separate frequency of the brain. All these people are looking to me as their squadron commander, I tell myself, and it is all very odd. Someone asks about how to evade shoulder-fired missiles. I answer the question, wondering meanwhile why no one is asking why I don't leave the squadron and hand the command over to someone who's actually familiar with the plane. I talk about what it means to move from a state of calm to a state of war. The rules for flight conduct and operational conduct are completely different, and here I'm harking back to my experience from the Six Day War, a war in which many of those in this room did not participate. Danny Pesach could take over the command, I say to myself, as I'm speaking to the assembled crowd. He's already been named the designated commander for the Skyhawk squadron that's due to be established at the Etzion base near Eilat. I wonder if I should tell them that I suggested to Ron that he replace me. No, it's not their business, and if I mention it I'll lose the little authority I currently possess. The way the people in this audience are speaking leaves no room for doubt—to them, I am the undisputed squadron commander. They want answers from me to their questions. For aren't you the pilot who not so long ago downed five enemy aircraft in three days? They want me to issue guidelines on operational matters. They even ask, in utmost earnestness, about matters requiring close familiarity with the plane, the kind of familiarity that for now I can only dream about.

I search the eyes of the older and more experienced reservist pilots for any hints of what they think I should really do. Glantz was my commander in the first stage of the pilots' course. Ilan Heit came together with me to be a pilot in the

Tel Nof Mirage squadron eight years ago. Pedo finished flight school four months after I got my wings. They and the other reservists sitting in the room know me. What do they think about this preposterous situation? In all of their eyes I read just one thing: Be our strong and clear commander. Don't look for any magic solutions. You stepped into Goldy's shoes due to tragic circumstances? That's your problem. From this moment forward, you are number one.

I scan the list of the call signs for the formation leaders. I am at the top of the list. Tzvika Bashan, the squadron's operations officer, has assigned me the call sign Peach, and from now until the end of the war, I will be Peach One.

Towards midnight, someone places a mattress in my office, and I lie down on it, not bothering to remove my flight suit or boots. At last I have time for a little talk with myself. *When you crossed the bay two months ago on the way to rescue Avi Lanir and Prigat,* says one half of my brain to the other half, *you felt that flying over Egyptian territory no longer triggered those awful symptoms that were always affecting you when you first returned to operational flying. Yeah, but then you were at least sitting in a Mirage,* retorts the half of the brain that was just listening up to now, *a plane that you knew inside out and with which you formed a single, smoothly functioning unit. Why?* both halves of the brain now ask in unison, *of all the people in the air force, have you been maneuvered into this situation in which you are starting a war from such a difficult spot, from such a problematic spot? Why, for god's sake, don't you just get up and go back to Hatzor Airbase and lead a Mirage formation into combat, something that you actually know how to do and do well?*

Never in my life have I shirked a mission, no matter what it is, I answer myself. *Everyone around me, above me and below me, expects me to command this squadron. And that is just what I intend to do. I intend to fly as much as I possibly can. Always more than anyone else in the squadron. I will fly mostly to Egypt, and I will prove, to myself first of all, that captivity is far behind me, that its grip on me is loosening and will soon be gone altogether.* And if I were a religious man, I would add the plea: May God make it so.

I can't fall asleep, just as I was unable to fall asleep when Sami turned off the light for me in solitary. I get up, go down to the operations room and start to get involved in the preparations for the second day of combat.

The next morning, the squadron takes part in Operation Tagar, planned as a day-long operation to attack the Egyptian surface-to-air missile batteries around the Canal. In the first flyover, several Egyptian air bases that could interfere with the big operation are also to be attacked. For my second-ever flight in a Skyhawk I put myself in a formation that is going to attack the Mansoura air base. My leader is Hanoch Pe'er from Netanya, and the first time I meet him and get to know him at all is at the 4:00 a.m. briefing.

Our target is the command bunker of the Egyptian air brigade responsible for the defense of the northeastern Nile Delta. This bunker is located less than three miles from Hajj el-Azz, the village near which I parachuted four years ago and from which I watched the trail of people snaking out to capture me. I tell myself that if I can pass this test, if I can fly over the place where I was hit and come back safely, it may help me later on.

When we take off, the sky is still dark, and here I am executing my first nighttime takeoff in a Skyhawk in a plane that is fully loaded with bombs and headed for an operational sortie. We quietly cross the Sinai Peninsula, the sun begins to rise at our backs when we're in the air, and the view of the ground brightens little by little. To us, Sinai is a familiar and friendly area, but it eventually comes to an end and now we're crossing the Suez Canal, at the northern end, at a low altitude, and entering straight into the Delta region. I feel no fear. Farmers are tilling the land, boats are cruising the canals—the Delta's pastoral appearance always manages to disguise the fact that this is war.

The tension must be rising as we approach the pull-up point, but the concentration needed to perform the correct actions usually overcomes the nerves and fear, enabling the pilot to fly even under the most extreme combat conditions. This time I drop my bombs on the first pass. The air brigade command is situated about half a mile south of the Mansoura air base, and when I come out and turn north, all of the airport's anti-aircraft fire is in front of me, creating that unfriendly gray red screen.

Hanoch heads out to the right while I decide to circumvent the flak from the west. I turn left, westward, into Egypt, only to find two MiG-21s ahead of me. I have an air-to-air missile and I want to shoot them down, but as my fingers are searching for the right button to push, it dawns on me that I don't know how to fire it. My guess is it must be the same button on the stick that I just used to release the bombs. But what has to change so that this button will also fire missiles?

I request assistance over the radio, and Yair Aloni, flying in the formation ahead of me, hears my question and tries to tell me what to do, but I still can't figure it out. In the Skyhawk there is a small needle-switch on the outside of the throttle. With a little flick of the pinkie it changes the bomb-release button into the missile-firing button. My attempt to understand Aloni's explanations and locate the tiny switch—while chasing after the two MiGs, with the anti-aircraft flak from Mansoura still on my tail—is hopeless. I have to let the MiGs go. I turn east and start my journey home.

I'm alone now, diving to zero altitude over the Delta, passing below the high-tension lines that stretch perpendicular to my flight path. The Delta ends and its eastern water channels drain into the Manzala wetlands. I turn north, over the sea, bypass Port Said to the north and turn northeast, towards Israel.

Eager to release all the tension that has built up in me, I maintain an altitude of about twenty yards above the sea, at the highest speed the plane can reach. I fly this way for about ten minutes, until I see Ashkelon just ahead. And then, in one swift move, I raise the nose vertically to the sky. Only when I reach 15,000 feet, and all of Israel is before me and Mansoura is far behind me, does a marvelous calm finally come over me, and I take myself back to Tel Nof.

Thirty-Seven

10-OCT-1973

Ehud Henkin was killed in his Phantom on the second day of the war in Syria. Ehud was my flight instructor in the final stage of the pilot training course, and was revered by all as a particularly gifted pilot. When I heard the news that evening I understood that we were in a war with new rules. If Henkin, in his super-advanced Phantom, was killed, then everything I believed up to now regarding flying in pressure situations no longer applied. And so I could also toss out the theory that someone who was hit before will be more susceptible to stress and perform less well on the battlefield, an idea the psychologists had presented to me following my captivity. Several more pilots in Henkin's league were hit and gravely wounded in the first two days of the war, and strangely enough, this had a calming effect upon me.

"Calm" probably isn't the right word to describe my feelings—better to say that it made me see that this war was not about to spare anyone, so nobody was going to bother about this or that fellow's special circumstances. My obligations as squadron commander, in these extreme conditions and in the unprecedented position in which I found myself, were all-consuming. It's hard to fully describe the relentlessly jam-packed schedule of a squadron commander in wartime, his absolutely total responsibility for the performance of his squadron. He hasn't a single moment for himself; his personal fate is as meaningless as a grain of sand. Perhaps it's the IDF mythology about what it means to be a commander. Perhaps it's the ethos upon which we were raised—to always excel in front of your subordinates, even if it means continually placing yourself in high-risk situations. Or perhaps it was just the workload entailed in commanding a complex combat unit when the reality facing you is so different and so much more brutal than ever predicted.

Whatever the reason, you completely empty yourself of any self-focus, and for me, when I thought about it later on, this was the magic key. The key that, after four years, seemed to help me unlock the chain that had kept me fettered to captivity's oppressive weight. And I went free.

Fear isn't something you talk about. At least not in the military.

The thought being that just talking about it introduces "noise in the system." Then there's the worry that talking about something that's basically emotional will just call attention to the fact that fear bears no correlation to military rank. Nor is it at all clear how well the words used by those talking about it would reflect their genuine feelings. And maybe there's really no need to talk about fear because, when you get right down to it, fighters are not tested on the fear scale. They are tested on the basis of their combat performance, in fear-inducing situations in which their lives are in danger. Not theoretical danger, the kind you discuss at a meeting in comfortable, air-conditioned and protected surroundings, but real and palpable danger. Danger that is glaringly obvious, whose implications are beyond all doubt. Not danger that may fade, as in a serious illness. Danger that means—to be or not to be. In which you are here at this moment but you may be gone the next. You cease to exist. You're history. Right this instant. This danger takes a myriad of forms in the arena in which the fighter operates.

So first and foremost, fear is something a person must grapple with alone. All that matters during a risky combat situation is whether or not the individual is able to maintain the needed performance level. And to hell with the question of fear.

There's no need to talk about it, also because after a while the way fear affects different members of the group starts to become apparent anyway. Words are superfluous, and explanations generally sound feeble, for whenever explanations are offered they are usually not needed.

All around me I note the first signs of a fear buildup in the fighters. It has many physical manifestations. Diarrhea, complaints of back pain, withdrawal and reduced communication with others, heightened sensitivity to criticism from other pilots about unsatisfactory performance during operational flights, the absence of the usual "When are you sending me on another mission?" keenness, and other examples that the experienced among us can easily spot in the very close quarters of the squadron building. The squadron commander must also deal with all of this, which immediately places him in the position of someone to whom such a thing couldn't happen, to whom it mustn't happen. He is above fear. He is immune. And thus, this pretense becomes the operative truth.

Deep down, I knew that every time I climbed the ladder up to the cockpit, I was hauling along the weight of having been hit and fallen captive. Flying, and combat aviation in particular, even in its wildest incarnations, is a process that is completely without external influences. Except for the turbulence everyone is familiar with from flying in stormy weather, an airplane operates in an environment that is entirely free of physical obstacles. There are none of those sensations that you find in driving, for instance, where the type of road you're on, bumps and potholes, moving from a paved to an unpaved surface and so on all make an impact. Flying is smooth and devoid of "friction."

Therefore, when a pilot's aircraft is hit, he experiences the blow like a burn to the flesh. The sensation I felt when my plane was hit has been with me at all times ever since that moment. My plane did not break apart in the air. It did not ignite and transform into a giant zooming fireball. There was just that brief dry thump, a sound that left no room for interpretation, and immediately afterward the aircraft's systems began to fail in rapid succession, just as the plane's manual, which I practically knew by heart, said they would. That single, unmistakable blow was all it took to make me aware that I was now sitting in a seven-ton hunk of metal hurtling through the sky that would no longer heed my commands.

This weight was with me wherever I went, especially when I flew, and most especially, whenever I flew a combat mission. It was with me all the time as I struggled to return to a top command position in the air force, and as time went by I had to find ways to lessen this weight. Strange as it might seem, I saw commanding the 115th Squadron in wartime as the ultimate opportunity for me to try to rid myself of this heavy ball and chain. The command appointment thrust me into an unfamiliar situation that I had to scramble to make sense of, but at the same time it gave me reassurance that there was no difference between me and the others, that there was no "added risk" attached to me just because I'd been hit, ejected and fallen into captivity. It was confirmation that I was back in the game of flying in danger and pressure situations, and I knew I was good at it.

The most frightening flight of my entire life turns out to be a rather routine strike—nothing heroic, nothing famous, not one of those flights about which admiring articles or stirring ballads are written. It is a sortie to attack an Egyptian armored unit that has crossed the Suez Canal near Qantara at the northern end and stationed itself on the eastern bank in order to defend the bridgehead.

It's the fourth day of the war, well into the initial phase of anxiety that has engulfed us. By now it is utterly clear that this is a "life or death" fight. I take off in the first formation, before sunrise, together with Yachin Kochava and Eitan Yeshayahu. The sun is just barely starting to light the eastern sky when, from quite a great distance, Kochava hurls his six cluster bombs, aiming to hit the exposed Egyptian troops and possibly neutralize them. Not only do Kochava's cluster bombs fail to kill the soldiers, their explosions serve as an alarm clock for the whole region.

Quick as a flash, a vertical red wall rises up on either side of the Canal. The sun is still low and has yet to reach full illumination, and countless Egyptian anti-aircraft shells are soaring upward, red tails streaking against the still dusky western sky. Everyone in the area is now firing up at us. And now Eitan and I are going after the dark tanks, which stand out in stark relief against the yellow dunes, and we are about to run head-on into the red wall.

I call, "Pulling!" and begin to climb. Before I reach the altitude where I plan to roll over to start the dive, two shoulder-launched missiles come whizzing at me from the western side of the Canal. I turn the plane's nose toward them to render them ineffective, and dive toward them. This is the way to avoid being hit by shoulder-launched missiles, whose power and impact depends upon them reaching the aircraft from the rear since they home in on the heat emitted from the engine. This evasive maneuver forces me across the Canal to the western side, so I make a hard turn left to return eastward. In so doing, I descend to an altitude of no more than a few dozen feet, and I can see hundreds, literally hundreds, of Egyptian soldiers lying on their backs and firing upward with their weapons, hoping to hit me perhaps.

I frantically weave my way past dozens of Egyptian armored vehicles until at last I cross back over the Canal. Now I'm on the eastern side again, winding between the dunes to get away as quickly as possible, and I make my way to the Tasa Junction in the northwestern part of the Sinai Peninsula, about thirty miles from the Canal, where Kochava and Eitan are waiting for me.

I am not supposed to go back and attack the same location a second time. "One pass and to the grass" is one of those phrases we were brought up on, and it originated in World War II. Those six little words are a distillation of combat experience acquired at the cost of hundreds, or likely thousands, of casualties. Meaning—execute one bombing pass and then get the hell out of there, flying "low to the grass." And absolutely, positively do not return to the place where the enemy is now waiting for you, guns at the ready.

But I still have all my bombs with me, and although I know it goes against procedure, I'm still the squadron commander and I cannot return to Tel Nof with my payload intact and create the appearance of a failure of nerve. I head out again with the two others watching me. This time I make it to the starting point for the dive at the Egyptian armored battalion, but the aim of the gunsight is so imprecise that I decide not to push the bomb-release button. The density of the flak is stunning. I've seen a lot of flak in my life, but never anything like this red spray that fills the air all around the battalion. If just one drop of this spray hits me the whole day will suddenly look quite different.

Now I'm back at Tasa Junction again, preparing to set out once more towards those same armored forces. To the south of us, on the shore of the Canal, a similar three-plane formation from our sister squadron at Tel Nof is using the same attack tactic. On my way to the Canal for the third time I see Yaniv Litani's plane from that configuration get hit, ignite and crash into the ground in a giant cloud of fire. I pull up for the third time, completely changing my manner of attack this time, climbing far beyond the altitude at which anti-aircraft flak is effective, even if this means increasing my exposure to the Egyptian surface-to-air missiles, just so I can finally execute this pass properly and drop my bombs.

I do.

My flight coverall is soaked through with perspiration, and it occurs to me that the Egyptians down below are probably remarking to one another—well, I guess these Zionist pilots aren't as clever as we were led to believe, if they keep coming back again and again. What the Egyptians don't know is that *I am the **squadron commander***, and that I will do anything on earth to bolster my authority and set the performance standard for my squadron.

I land at Tel Nof, already wiped out at six in the morning, and worse, deeply concerned about the risky and problematic method we were handed the night before by the air force's operations division. In the air on my way back home I'd already altered the attack method for the three-plane formations from my squadron that were coming after me to the tactic I'd adopted—i.e., climbing high above the anti-aircraft flak prior to the strike, with one plane in the formation keeping an eye out for missile launches.

As soon I get back on the ground, I try to get the other squadrons to make this change. No one has time to talk to me. They're all busy preparing for a strike on the general staff headquarters in Damascus (a flight about which many articles will later be written), and the Canal remains an issue for each squadron commander to deal with as he chooses.

Ehud Shelah, commander of the parallel squadron to mine at Tel Nof, is killed at seven-thirty that morning. He is killed not far from where I was attacking just two hours before and is the fifth pilot not to return in those two hours. Two have been killed, two have been taken captive and one is later rescued. The air force calls a halt to this mode of attack and shifts to a different one.

Though this is still just my fourth day in command, I've added another very tricky flight to my Skyhawk resume, and more importantly, I've started to really become the authority that defines the squadron's manner of operation, and all because *I was physically there myself.*

The ability to overcome fear in the midst of war is a most fascinating thing. There's no magic to it; it doesn't involve any psychological exercise or voodoo incantations. It comes from personal reckoning, the cohesiveness of the unit and, above all, the strength of the commander and the personal example he sets. From this perspective, the war should have served as the final step in my quest to erase the memory of my captivity.

Thirty-Eight

10-OCT-1973

A t night I go to bed in one of the empty apartments in the family quarters on the base, an old apartment that isn't in use and has been put at my disposal. I have no trouble falling asleep. I am so weary that I'm out like a light the second I lie down.

I sleep for two or three hours, and then it comes. The dream that hasn't visited me for more than a month. It is intensely vivid. This time I'm being chased along the bank of a river that's lined on either side by beautiful palm trees. *How did I end up in Iraq?* I wonder, so far from Israel. I surmise that this is either the Tigris or the Euphrates, which means that even if I manage to elude my pursuers, as my fleeing self is always so desperate to do in the first part of the dream, I have no way to get back to Israel. I sprint between the palm trees and when I glance backward, I see that my pursuers are not running like I am. They are just leisurely strolling along, they seem to be smiling even, and display no air of urgency. I shift my gaze forward, trying to see where this riverbank path upon which I am now racing like a madman is leading. There's nothing there, just an endless darkness waiting to swallow up anyone who comes near. I run and run and then, just as I'm about to hit a dead end, I activate my self-waking technique.

The physical agitation that accompanies this self-waking—rapid breathing, perspiration, racing pulse—is stronger than ever this time. I sit up, only to find myself in a bed that is completely foreign to me. I've been sleeping on an iron-framed military bed, covered with a sheet made of some peculiar type of green paper I've never seen before, and two army-issue wool blankets on top of that. I haven't a clue as to who has been looking after this vacant apartment or made this bed. But it's an alien environment and when I get out of bed, I decide to go to the fridge for a glass of milk to help me calm down.

I enter the apartment's kitchen for the first time since I started using the place to snatch a tiny bit of sleep here and there. It's the original kitchen from when this place was built fifteen years ago and evidently hasn't been used in a very long time. It's very small. There are cracks in the countertop on either side of the sink, and inside the sink, a cockroach is madly scurrying back and forth—God knows how long the thing has been trapped there. The cupboard doors below the counter are painted turquoise—the exact shade of turquoise as my cell door in Abbasiya Prison in Cairo. The plastic door handles are mostly broken. A feeling of misery overtakes me. Of course—there is no fridge, no milk, no nothing.

I put on the flight coverall and the gray wool military socks and sit down outside on the stoop by the door. Just like Sami used to sit on the steps outside my room at the prison on nights when Aziz and Sayeed were interrogating me.

It's 3:00 a.m., darkness and quiet all around; no fighter jets are taking off and no helicopters are coming in to land after an operation in Sinai. I try to play psychologist and figure out whether the dream was triggered by the complexity and high risk of the morning's flight with Kochava and Eitan, or whether it's just another ordinary visit from one of these dreams. Later in the day I had done two more bombing passes. At 11:30 a.m., I attacked near the city of Suez and towards sunset I led a four-plane formation to attack armored forces along the "Chronicle" axis, as it's called on the code maps. Both of these missions were very straightforward and didn't entail the slightest trace of that feeling from the early morning sortie, when I was sure I was about to be hit. They should have brought me back to war in its most basic form—namely that not every attack is a matter of "to be or not to be." But then along comes the dream as if to say, *The scars of captivity shall not be erased.*

The temperature has dropped steeply on this October night and the cold cuts right through the coverall's thin gray fabric. I zip it all the way up and hug myself, trying to vanquish the nighttime chill, but it's no use. I can feel my body getting colder and colder, but I want a few more minutes of quiet before I must return to reality and turn my attention to the flight missions for the coming morning. When I feel my feet starting to go numb, I go back inside the apartment, lace up my boots, wash my face, put on my flying jacket and head down to the squadron. For now, the squadron building is the closest thing to a warm home that I can go back to.

Thirty-Nine

13-OCT-1973

The three combat squadron commanders meet with Ron Konen, the base commander, at the base command post. The time is 4:00 a.m.

In a very short while our counterattack on the Golan Heights will begin, after we were driven nearly to the brink there. We're sitting in the underground room that's used for giving briefings. The walls are covered with maps, but my faith in the intelligence maps has steadily eroded since the start of the war. Something has gone seriously wrong with military intelligence's ability to supply us with a detailed and accurate picture of what's happening in the war, and a wise person would take care to come up with his own intelligence assessment, or at least regard the one he's given with some skepticism. I don't look at the maps.

My eyes scan the room. I'm studying the people who are sitting silently in this small, cramped space, waiting for

Ron, who is due to arrive any minute. Opposite me sits Eliezer (Leizik) Prigat, commander of the base's Phantom squadron, the 119th. Leizik seems somehow older than the other squadron commanders and gives the impression that he might even be a little too old for this whole war business. But in fact he is commanding this terrific squadron in a way that is nothing less than noble.

To his right sits Giora Oren, Ron's deputy who oversees the base's day-to-day operations. His eyes are bloodshot and he is unshaven. Ever since I can recall, his eyes have been red, for he grew up on a farm, and from the time he was very young began rising at 4:00 a.m. to help his father with the chores before going to school, and then as soon as he got home set to work learning how to take apart and repair anything composed of two or more parts. Since the start of the war, I haven't caught him sleeping once.

I don't see Shmulik Benrom, my friend from the pilot training course. Yesterday he took over for Ehud Shelah, who was killed the day before that. Ron summoned Shmulik from his place as a Phantom pilot in the 119th Squadron, and he must now be busy quickly retraining to fly the Skyhawk and bracing himself for the heavy turbulence of commanding a squadron in wartime.

Also sitting in the room are the base's intelligence officer and the operations officer. These men are not pilots and their chairs are placed slightly behind ours. They regard us with a mix of admiration and awe, and maybe also a drop of pity.

I think about how at this very moment dozens of groups like this one are meeting all over the war zone, from Mount Hermon in the north to the southern tip of the Sinai Peninsula, trying to plan for the coming day of combat. How to make it maximally effective while guarding their soldiers' lives. In my mind's eye I see the small clusters of commanders huddling together, cheeks stubbly and hair disheveled, in sweat-soaked and sand-coated khakis, clutching blue plastic cups from which they sip bitter black coffee to help them survive on just three hours sleep (Who, I wonder, is the person who amid all the chaos of war is able to arrange for coffee at 4:00 a.m. on some godforsaken dune in the Sinai desert?), and I know that they, and we here—the commanders of combat units—are the real backbone of the military. In the end, it is we who cause the plans to be executed, as we ram our heads, and those of our men, straight into the walls of fire seeking to stop us.

The iron door opens and Ron walks in. I've known Ron since my early days in uniform, and have served under his command for most of my years in the air force. His expression is grim. He is commanding the air force's largest and most complex air base, and must be operating on very little sleep. He returned around midnight from a meeting with the air force commander, grabbed just a few hours' rest at most, and now here he is, preparing to brief us for the sixth day of combat. I continue observing him. His flight coverall, with the insignia on the shoulders and the base's symbol sewn more or less over the heart, is pristine. His black boots are as shiny as Anwar's flight boots were. Ron is one of those officers who attach great importance to the uniform. He will never—ever—be caught looking anything less than flawless. For him, service in the air force is an all-encompassing calling that entails achievements, satisfactions, commitments—in short, everything, and the always crisp uniform says, "I am here to do my job as perfectly as I am dressed." His eyes look smaller than normal now and his hair is not as glossy as usual. No question about it, a very heavy weight is resting on his shoulders, and he is bearing it in a way that, years later, will make air force commander Benny Peled remark in his oh-so-British style, "Ron was the best field commander I ever had."

Ron begins to speak. His voice is a deep baritone. The key to gauging Ron's state of mind lies in the pitch of his voice. It can reach as high as a soprano range when he gets carried away telling funny stories—often about himself. But when his voice plunges to the lower octaves, only a fool would dare utter a word, let alone try to divert the conversation or discussion with some clever comment meant to dispel the tension. No way—not a word. Not a sound. Now his deep baritone is not wavering in the least. No one here would dream of interrupting him.

The incursion into Syria gets underway this morning, over the borderline from the start of the war. The plan calls for each squadron to be assigned a sector of responsibility, an area that it must "cleanse" ahead of the armored units' planned eastward advance. My squadron, the 115th Squadron, is assigned the "America" axis, the central artery connecting Quneitra with Damascus. Another day of arduous combat is about to begin, but at least there is one bright spot. Air force intelligence reports that the Syrian surface-to-air missile batteries are no longer active and that it is finally possible to fly comfortably at high altitude beyond the reach of the ordinary anti-aircraft flak, to identify targets and efficiently attack them.

I go back to the squadron building, grab a cup of coffee and enter the briefing room. The room is crammed with pilots sitting there hunched in their flight jackets against the early morning chill, waiting to hear what form our sixth day of combat will take. I explain the plan of action and, like every other morning, I head out as the leader of the first formation.

Just as I'm boarding the bus for the underground shelter, Nili the operations room secretary comes running after me. "Ron's on the phone. He wants to talk to you."

"Nili, I'm already on the bus."

"He insists, Giora, he must speak with you." On the porch I see "Bambi" Ofer, the leader of the second pair.

"Bambi," I say to him, "You lead the first pair and I'll take off after you." I finish speaking with Ron about further missions for the squadron that day in the Egyptian sector, take Miki Schneider, my number two, with me, and hurry on my way so I can take off on time, exactly ten minutes behind Bambi. When we're over Hadera, Yitzhak Tor, Bambi's number two, calls Peach One over the squadron's private radio channel.

"They fired two missiles at us," he says. "One of them hit Number One and he blew up in midair." Tor sounds shaken by what he has just seen. I instruct him to return to the base, while I continue on toward the Golan Heights. We were told there were no missiles. If there was a change, the attack controller would surely have informed me. Is it possible that a single stubborn missile battery remains? But now I'm on the radio attack channel and the controller is not reporting any change in the overall picture of the situation. Could the missiles have been launched from one lone and determined Syrian battery?

By now I'm approaching the Sea of Galilee and the attack controller starts giving me the coordinates for my target. It's an artillery battery next to the village of Khan Arnabah, northeast of Quneitra. The morning is crystal clear and Quneitra is in plain sight as we get closer. I run my eyes along the black road that runs eastward from Quneitra towards Damascus—the "America" axis, spot the village of Khan Arnabah to the north and the narrow road that connects it to the "America" axis, and gradually focus my gaze upon the area where the artillery battery is situated. "Eye contact with the target," I tell Miki Schneider. Quneitra is now behind us and the Syrian side of the Golan Heights is spread out before us, quiet and seemingly unthreatening.

Now I see the battery itself, with its six artillery trenches, and I begin the rightward roll at 15,000 feet in order to dive and execute the bombing pass. And then I see them. Three balls of fire trailing three snakelike plumes of white smoke speeding toward us from the right side of the plane, from the east, from a Syrian missile battery on the other side of Tel Hara. For a fraction of a second, they look like the anonymous faces that chase me in my dreams, from which there is never any escape.

"Break!" I shout over the radio, rolling right in the direction of the three SA6 missiles and lowering the plane's nose to gain energy for the evasive maneuvers. The fireballs and their smoky tails are coming toward us at a tremendous velocity, spread out like a three-fingered fan. I hit the chaff switch—releasing a spray of tiny, radar-fooling metal fragments to hopefully confuse the missile which is almost certainly locked in on me, as I maneuver wildly to try to avoid being hit.

"Your tail is on fire," says an anonymous voice on the radio. I swivel my head around far enough to see the tail of my aircraft but I don't see any fire. But then, in the midst of turning my plane, I see Miki's plane high above me. It's a breathtaking sight. The plane is plummeting vertically to the ground. The front half looks just like an ordinary Skyhawk, but from the mid-fuselage back it's a huge flaming torch forty or fifty yards long that is billowing like the scarf of a pilot flying one of those old-fashioned open-cockpit planes.

Cries of "Eject!" are heard over the radio. "Eject! Eject! Eject!" I cannot spot any parachute and have no idea if Miki managed to eject or not. I keep breaking from side to side, completing my dive down to very low altitude and heading back west toward the Israeli part of the Golan Heights. I take a few deep breaths to try to get my nerves under control again. My heart is beating wildly and sweat is pouring down my back.

"Peach Two was hit by a missile," I report to the attack controller. I see now that, contrary to the intelligence assessment, the area is teeming with missiles, and the plan of attack I gave my pilots at the briefing this morning is no longer applicable or feasible.

But this is the counterattack into Syria, which just a few days ago was seriously threatening Tiberias and the Hula Valley north of the Sea of Galilee, and we will continue to press the attack, as full partners with the ground forces, although we shall have to go about it another way. More pairs from the squadron, spaced ten minutes apart, are on their way north. Obviously, once again we're in a situation where the mode of operation handed down by the air force command does not match the reality being experienced by those who are actually out there in the field.

I hear the voices of Ilan Heit, the leader of the next pair, and Dudi Kenneth, his Number Two, coming over the attack channel now, and right after comes the voice of Gadi Ullman from Kibbutz Na'an, leading his pair. I order the two pairs from my squadron to stop where they are in the air, and over the squadron radio channel I explain the situation, order a return to the method of attacking at low altitude, and coordinate all the necessary changes with the duty operations officer in the squadron operations room. Once I finish putting this new tactic in place while circling between Kiryat Shemona and Quneitra, I go unleash my fury in an attack, from a low altitude this time, on the artillery battery in Khan Arnabah, which I was prevented from bombing earlier.

Now I'm at high altitude, alone without Miki, without Peach Two, heading back home to the squadron. Bambi Ofer and Miki Schneider are the squadron's sixth and seventh casualties in six days.

The way back to Tel Nof is long enough to give me time to think about myself as well. My previous sorties in the war were no walk in the park, but having those three Syrian missiles zooming right at me and watching Peach Two go down has made me wonder if the gamble I'm taking isn't crazy, isn't totally beyond reason. Learning to operate this new aircraft in the midst of fierce combat, commanding a squadron I barely know, grappling with the residue of my POW experience and my uncertainty about the ability of my right leg and left arm to withstand another ejection—Is this really an acceptable way to be operating?

I think about my commanders in the air force. Would Benny Peled fly in my condition? Would Rafi and Ivri be able to fly if they were in my situation? And Forman? And Amos? And Yalo? Ron may have had an experience slightly similar to mine near the end of the War of Attrition, but a much more moderate version. So much more moderate that there's really no comparison. Agassi is considered an especially brave pilot. If he were in my shoes, after everything I've been through in the past four years, would he fly?

Herzliya is below me now and as I begin to descend in preparation for landing, over the red radio I hear the leader of the pair that followed me reporting a successful execution of his attack. It appears that the low-altitude approach could be the right way to avoid the missiles and to help Raful and Ori Orr, the leading commanders of the armored forces, advance eastward. My thoughts return to the war. I must get to the squadron's operations room to try to find a way to improve our performance and to ensure that we're doing our part in the best way possible.

On the ride back to the squadron building after landing I think about Schneider. Was he killed? Is he alive? And if he's alive, did he survive in one piece, unscathed by that massive blazing torch that moments before was one of the squadron's aircraft? I know him as a young pilot and as a gentle type. How will he cope with captivity? Will he adopt the "I am a pilot, I am a lieutenant, I am an officer in the Israeli Air Force" attitude and survive? Or does the Sudanese giant who pummeled me for two nights in a row in solitary confinement in Abbasiya Prison in Cairo have a clone in Damascus, which will make it even harder for him to get through the horrible experience that awaits him? And what about all the others in the squadron? A week ago I'd never met these pilots and didn't even know their names, and now I am the one responsible for them. How can I properly command Eldar and Reisman and Gur and Avner Ra'anan, and all their comrades, who've become the flesh of my flesh?

I erase from my thoughts the whole discussion of which of my commanders in the air force would have done what I am doing. My guess is that they wouldn't have, but they were never called upon to do so, so it isn't fair to contemplate the question at all. As the Jewish funeral prayer says, each one of us will have to "stand for his fate at the End of Days." Myself included. And when that time comes I will be judged, for one thing, on the way that I commanded the squadron in this brutally difficult war. I know that this test is only going to get harder and harder, but I have no intention of giving up.

The bus brings me from the underground shelter to the squadron building. I strip off my flight gear and hang it on the designated hanger, take a sack of milk from the fridge and go down to the operations room. In addition to leading the squadron in the air, I must lead it to make the necessary changes each day in our mode of combat. This is what will enable us to fight in the optimum way amid the ever-changing reality we are facing. A crucial key to success in wartime is the ability to note, and adjust to, the discrepancies between the world for which you trained and the world in which you actually find yourself when a war happens. This is the test of every commander of every rank, both intellectually and intuitively, and it is upon this that his glory or ignominy depends. I know that, beyond the combat missions in which I am personally engaged, this is the weightiest task facing me as a commander.

Later that night, when I'm on my way to the command group meeting with the base commander, the intelligence officer calls me to report that Miki Schneider has just been interviewed on Radio Damascus. *They know about you. They'll get you home. It'll be okay.* I say to him in my heart.

Forty

16-OCT-1973

On the afternoon of October 16, I am making my way back from the Suez Canal to Tel Nof, a trip that takes about twenty to twenty-five minutes. A span of time that seems quite brief for someone used to measuring the journey from the far side of the Sinai Peninsula back to Israel in ground-transportation terms. But for someone used to doing it in the air, it is plenty long, and feels much, much longer to someone who has just attacked over the Suez Canal as part of the effort to repel the Egyptians and is now in a rush to get back to base, who must quickly digest this mission that was just carried out and think about what comes next in the lead-up to the incursion into Egypt.

Amid all the chatter on the radio I hear the controller call for Ampere One. This type of call is familiar to me by now. It's a call over the emergency channel and what it means is that Ampere formation is on its way home to land, but Ampere One is not responding over the radio. Ampere One may be having a technical problem that prevents him from responding. But Ampere One may also not be responding simply because he is no longer sitting in the cockpit of his aircraft.

The emergency channel enables pilots who've ejected and reached the ground safely to make contact using the radio that is part of their emergency gear, and to report on their situation. The procedure is for the control units to try to raise the pilot who is in trouble, and this is what anyone who was on the emergency channel could now hear. The calls for Ampere One are repeated over and over at the standard rate, and it's clear to me that this pilot has been hit. The aircraft's radio control dial has several positions, and it would be very easy to just move it one click to the left, to shut off the emergency channel and quietly make my way home. After all, there's nothing I can do to help solve this problem.

I don't know who Ampere One is yet I can't stop listening, as I pray all the while that by the time I reach Tel Nof I will hear him respond and know that even if he did abandon his aircraft, he is still alive and will soon be rescued. The calls for Ampere One accompany me all the way to Kiryat Gat, where I must switch to the channel for the Tel Nof control tower ahead of the landing process. I am forced to leave the mystery of Ampere One unresolved.

When I get back to the operations room, I ask Ora, the operations room secretary, to find out for me who Ampere One is, then I immediately get busy going over our next flights for that day. I'm in the midst of a phone call with Brigadier General Yehezkel Somekh, the most senior air force officer in the Southern Command. He's been monitoring the attack that I just led and phoned me directly to give me coordinates for more targets west of the Canal that he wants us to attack. We're examining targets on the Sirius code map, the map that will become the common denominator for all the combat in Egypt, and it's an animated conversation.

Ora puts down the telephone receiver she was speaking on, waits patiently for me to finish, and when her eyes meet mine, she tells me, "Ampere One is someone by the name of Menachem Eyal from the 102nd Squadron."

My blood freezes in my veins. For Ora, it's just 'someone by the name of Menachem Eyal,' but for me it's Menachem, my best friend since the age of fourteen. Together we attended the military boarding school adjacent to the Reali High School in Haifa, together we went to the pilot training course, together we got our wings and together we spent a large portion of our after-hours leisure time. I remained in the air force and Menachem left the military and became a pilot for El Al. Now I'm here after another landing and Menachem is Ampere One, who isn't responding over the emergency channel, and I don't know if he's somewhere out there fighting for his life, or if he's already dead.

The war enters its eleventh day and we resume fighting mainly on the Egyptian front. Yesterday and the day before that I attacked two Egyptian Air Force bases: Al-Salahiya Airbase north of Ismailiya and Al-Quatamiya Airbase, located in the desert midway between the city of Suez and Cairo. Odd as it may sound, I liked these types of missions. The strikes on the Egyptian forces around the Canal were a bit vague in a way—it wasn't plain to see how they served the greater purpose or how well they were in tune with the issues facing the ground forces.

Clearly, our side is having trouble defining targets of high value, a problem that derives perhaps from the difficulty of grasping the overall combat scenario. This problem is evident in the tentative pace with which worthy targets are designated, and in the doubts that begin to creep into us as to whether we are really helping where we are needed most and can have an impact. The Egyptian air bases, on the other hand, are clear-cut targets, even though they are much more massively defended.

As I lead my formation of four planes, following Glantz's formation, to bomb Al-Quatamiya, I feel I am about to deal the Egyptian Air Force a severe blow. This is my third attack on an Egyptian air base, and beyond the purpose it serves in the war, I also feel like I have a personal score to settle. I do not intend to miss a single opportunity to try to even the score.

When we get there, the anti-aircraft fire on the southern side of Al-Quatamiya air base is very lively, for Glantz's formation has just attacked before us and stirred it to life. We come under fire as soon as we pull up, but I notice that I am almost completely free of fear. I feel a moment of euphoria when I drop my bombs on my assigned target. And when I gather the formation together after the bombing pass to head southeast back to the desert, towards the Suez Bay and then home, I say over the radio in Arabic, "*Aziz, hadha minshanak*" (Aziz, this is for you), fantasizing that Egyptian intelligence is eavesdropping on our radio channel. None of the other pilots understand these words they hear on the radio, and they are so incongruous, so far removed from our normal radio patter, that I am not even questioned about them during the post-mission briefing.

When we start to climb high, after crossing the Suez Canal on the way home, and I am still surging with adrenaline from the satisfaction of having led such a long and successful flight in Egyptian territory, and from the excitement of diving into the anti-aircraft flak and precisely dropping my bombs on the specific MiG-21 reinforced concrete shelter I was assigned at the start of the runway in Al-Quatamiya—that "king of the sky" feeling comes back to me. This attack took place in the early morning hours, there is still a whole day of fighting ahead of us, and I am already eager to get back to the squadron, both to oversee the operations and, as I am subconsciously aware, to calm myself down from the "high" that has just come over me.

Forty-One

OCT-1973

The war goes on. Our consciousness is now divided in two—struggling to absorb the shock waves of the past eleven days and at the same time striving to find ways for us to fly better, more effectively and more safely. The squadron is a blend of nonstop activity and signs of fatigue that are beginning to appear with some pilots. We haven't yet reached the critical state where a pilot actually has trouble flying, but at our end-of-the-day meetings the more veteran fellows among us can tell just who is in need of special attention.

By now I am the unchallenged squadron commander. The circumstances under which I received the command have begun to be filed under "formerly supernatural events, now seemingly natural" and daily life has acquired the typical character of an air force command position—i.e., a highly centralized command style. Nothing is done without the squadron commander's involvement, and absolutely no changes are made to the spirit of things that he continually dictates by his presence and by his ability to formulate instructions and orders. My grace period is already a distant memory, and as time goes on I am gaining the pilots' trust regarding the manner in which I am leading the squadron.

Still, they never for a moment relent in insisting that this path be well-defined, clearly worded and, above all, backed up each morning anew by my personal example in combat. At the same time, the feeling is intensifying that the bonds developing here will last for many years to come, being the kind that grow out of the unique experience of fighting a war together. The ceaseless traffic of pairs of pilots or four-man teams—being given their mission, donning their flight gear and then, armed with maps and aerial photos, descending the steps from the front porch of the squadron building to board the bus that will take them to their planes—has become an ordinary sight, just as the their departure for training flights had been until recently.

I watch them as they move about—veteran pilots Shimon Heller and Asher Ne'eman; Rafi Lev who got married two days before the war broke out; David Noy and Dov Perry, who at first looked too young to be fighting—now they all seem much more serious and grown-up than they did on the first day that I met them.

In the dressing room, certain compartments stand deserted: That of Shimon Ash, a serious older fellow whom I didn't get to speak with at all before he was hit and went missing; of Mario Shaked, a special blend of El Al pilot and Italian baron; of Yisrael Rosenblum, the young man who requested to be sent to attack in the Golan Heights because he hailed from nearby Kibbutz Hagoshrim, and when I sent him there, was hit by a missile and killed; of Tzvika Bashan, the operations officer and star of the squadron. When the attack controller gave Tzvika his target at the Canal, I was in the air on the same radio channel and listened until I heard the words, "One, you're all on fire!"; and of Bambi Ofer, who took my place on the start of the fifth day of fighting and was hit by a missile directly over Outpost 109 in the Golan Heights.

We know that Miki Schneider and Tzvika Rosen are in captivity and we're hoping that perhaps one of the others whose fate is unknown right now will turn out to also be in captivity and that we will get to see him again one day. For now, we've parked their cars in the far corner of the squadron parking lot and Kobi the adjutant, who is back with us, with the help of Miri, the squadron office secretary, packed up their personal items and left them in their assigned spaces.

Now I have a field bed set up in the squadron commander's office, so I can spend as much time as I want in the air, in the operations room or in any of the other squadron facilities at any time of day or night. At last I've found time to get to know the ground crew, both the regular conscripts and the reservists. They seem to be vying for the chance to work more and more, knowing that everything we accomplish in the air is thanks to them and their boundless dedication on the ground.

Sometimes, when I feel the need to get away for a few hours in order to come back new and fresh, I go to nap in that derelict apartment in the family quarters, on that bed with the green paper sheets and those wool blankets you can never get away from in the military. I lie there, fearing at first that the dream might return as it did that time after the flight in which I stubbornly returned to attack the same target three times. But the dream doesn't come, and the only thing that disturbs my sleep is the jangle of the operations telephone that is shared by four different houses in the family quarters and used to wake and summon pilots in accordance with the flight plans of the various squadrons.

On the fourteenth day of the war, as it's getting dark, I get into Goldy's car—now my car. Goldy's tragic death in a training accident, just three days before the war, has been obscured now by the war and its casualties. From all I've heard about him in the squadron, he was a truly outstanding person, and I hope that he will receive the recognition he deserves.

I drive to Tel Aviv to my parents' house to see my family before I plan to visit some of the families of the missing. Driving through the pitch-blackness of the country, the way it is these nights, comes as a shock. Up to now I haven't had a moment to think about how life looks "on the outside." The thought strikes me that the total darkness through which I am making my way from Tel Nof to my parents' home is not due merely to the lack of lighting in the streets and houses, but that this darkness has a much deeper meaning. An impenetrable gloom has descended upon the basic assumptions of our life here, and there is no telling how long it will be until someone is able to restore the light.

I ring the bell at my parents' house. I don't recall who opens the door, but Netta is standing there too. She is two and a half years old, and for about five seconds she stares at me wide-eyed, in apparent disbelief. I snatch her up in my arms and take her outside to the lawn without anyone following us.

I know that of all the people in the house right now, she is the only one who will not be able to remember me should I be killed tomorrow morning or the day after that or the day after that or on any other day until this war is over. I clutch her to my chest, unable to say a word to her. I pace back and forth on the grass with her, holding her close, and still there is total silence between us. When my emotions settle down a little, I hold her a little bit away from me so I can gaze at her face and etch it into my memory. Finally, I muster the strength to ask her how she is doing.

She doesn't answer. She just stares at me for a minute with her big dark eyes. Then she lays her head back down on my right shoulder and, seemingly of its own accord, her left hand slips into place on my other shoulder, right in the little space between the epaulets and the shirt, where it always likes to go, and I feel her five tiny fingers. The fingers do not rest there mutely, as if I am some stranger. They rub and massage my shoulder, wordlessly saying: *I remember you. I know who you are. Why did you disappear all of a sudden? Why are we living with Grandma and Grandpa? And why is everybody so serious all the time?*

I keep walking back and forth with her on the lawn, aware that everyone is watching me through the large glass sliding door that runs the length of the living room, and not caring. The little fingers have more to say to me, *Don't go away again. Don't leave me again. Please.*

Slowly, I go back inside the house. Everybody is there. Miriam, my parents, Miriam's parents, and for the first time it hits me that they never imagined that I was actually flying in this war. They'd been relying the whole time on what Miriam was told on the first day: There was no way I could be flying now that I was commanding a squadron whose aircraft I'd never flown before.

I'm not sure exactly what we talked about in the half-hour I spent with them, I just remember that it was a halting and guarded conversation. A conversation between two different universes. Everyone else in the room was still part of the familiar universe that was also mine just two weeks ago, while I now hailed from a new, parallel universe whose inhabitants' lives would constantly remain on the line until quiet prevailed once again.

Eventually, my father starts inquiring about some of my friends whom my parents know well. When I say, in answer to the question I fervently prayed would not be asked, that Menachem Eyal is missing, my father clutches the left side of his chest with both hands, gets up from his chair and walks to the far side of the room, muttering words that I cannot make out. He turns around and comes back, hands now pressing his temples, and I realize that I cannot stay here any longer.

I hug everyone goodbye, especially my mother and father, and all understand that I must now return to my universe, a universe they could never possibly fathom. Miriam and Netta escort me outside, Miriam quietly clinging to my arm. I get in the car and they bend down to the window. Miriam bids me farewell with the same words she has used a thousand times before (and will use thousands more times in the years to come), "Take care of yourself."

I look at them once more, one last time for that visit, and then I start driving to Menachem Eyal's home in Ramat Hasharon. I try to think whether I am really taking care of myself, and if so, how. We both know full well that avoiding flying in the war is not an option. Just how the bloody hell do you "take care of yourself" in a war?

With these thoughts running through my head, I enter the Eyals' house. Menachem's whole family is there. His parents, his two brothers and his sister, and of course his wife Orka and their three small children. On the face of it, the Eyal family's universe also resembles that stable, quiet and secure universe we all knew until recently. But again, just like in my parents' house, out of all the people there, it is the father who gives outward expression to just how excruciating the situation is.

"Bring Menachem back to me!" he cries out suddenly, "I want Menachem!" probably already aware deep down that Menachem is never coming back.

A few months after the war, Menachem's body was found next to his plane.

It's nearly midnight when I find myself driving, fairly slowly, back to the Tel Nof base. The night is very dark and the moon has long passed its zenith, following its westward path to set in tandem with the rising sun in the east. This is my first chance to really contemplate the war, not in concrete terms of how to fight more effectively, but in more abstract terms.

From my military boarding school I took the lesson that whatever the mission assigned to you, or whatever mission you have taken on, it must be accomplished in full.

From the air force, and from the 119th Squadron in particular, with which I fought in the Six Day War, I took the lesson that merely accomplishing the mission is not sufficient. You must strive to accomplish it as perfectly as possible.

And from my father I took the lesson that if accomplishing the mission entails self-humiliation, unsavory deeds or a blatant disregard of principles, then one should think twice about whether achieving this aim is worth the bad taste it will leave for a long time to come.

I conclude that Israel is faced with a mission that it has no choice but to complete. The execution will not be perfect. That is clear. How does this square with my father's principles? On a night when a fierce all-out war is raging between us and our enemies, I cannot yet say.

Nor can I say anything about the Israel Defense Force or the Israeli Air Force. The vantage point of the wartime squadron commander who is constantly in the eye of the storm is very limited, and one must be leery of getting carried away with statements that have no factual basis, as I already sense is happening in the media.

But I can think about my squadron, the 115th Squadron, in terms of those principles. The 115th Squadron will fulfill its missions. So we have done up to now and no power in the world will prevent us from continuing to do our part in the war, whatever is assigned to us. Will we do it perfectly? No, surely not. The seven planes we've lost so far are more than proof enough that our execution is not perfect. We must keep striving to improve. We must never for a moment be fully satisfied with ourselves. We must desire to do better. Have we humiliated ourselves at any point? No, thank god, no. I am coming to deeply love the men of the squadron, and brimming with pride over the way in which they are fighting.

Such thoughts occupy me for quite a while. Now I am passing through the city of Rehovot, all the way from the Weizmann Institute in the north to the Yemenite Sha'arayim neighborhood in the south. The city is as desolate as a ghost town in one of those movies set in a post-nuclear holocaust world. Not even a single cat is prowling the streets it seems. The whole time I'm driving through the city something seems off to me, but I can't put my finger on it. Not until I start to get beyond the more heavily populated section of town do I realize what's been bothering me. The car headlights. The headlights of the cars parked silently along the curbs were all painted blue. They were painted blue so that their lights would not be seen from the air. *It's to keep enemy pilots from being able to identify the place*, I think. *What an incredibly well-organized country we are. But wait—I'm a pilot, too. And we have nighttime attack plans in the countries where we fight. And I don't recall us ever devising a plan based on the headlights in Cairo, or Alexandria, or Damascus, or Suez, or any other city.* Painting headlights to camouflage them, usually in blue, was common practice in World War II. That's what they did when they tried to protect London, and Coventry, and Berlin, and maybe Tokyo. But aviation has seen major technological advances since then that have completely changed the face of air combat. And here we are still painting the headlights blue. Somebody from the government must have come on the radio or television and solemnly instructed the citizenry to paint their car headlights blue. Countless cans of blue paint somehow appeared and legions of good people, inhabitants of the parallel universe, went about the task of painting their headlights with utmost gravity, surely feeling that they were doing their part in the war effort. *So the state is still thinking in World War II terms. What other aspects of our military thinking have remained frozen, stuck in an irrelevant past reality, supposedly yielding effective action but actually being more akin to running in place, if not going backwards?*

At the intersection near the entrance to the Tel Nof base I pick up three hitchhikers. They are reservists, somewhat older guys, from the Tel Nof construction unit, the ones whose job it is to repair the runways should they be damaged in an aerial attack. They ride with me in silence, and each one of us seems to have quite a weight on his mind.

When I arrive at the squadron building I feel like I've found my way back from the other universe to the universe I've called home for the past two weeks. I have no intention of making this transition again, not until the end of the war. When the war is over, the two universes will get together once more, lick their wounds and reunite.

I am so bushed that I go straight to my room. Over the intercom I ask Uri Margalit, the combat manager on duty, if there's anything I need to know. The orders for tomorrow have not yet arrived, he informs me. Don't wake me until four in the morning, I tell him, and when I lie down on the mattress in my room, I'm asleep before my head hits the pillow.

EPILOGUE

After the attack on Al-Quatamiya, I decided I would do all my fighting exclusively on the Egyptian front.

On the Arab radio broadcasts, on Radio Damascus and Radio Cairo, as a result of information gleaned from POW interrogations, I was named as the commander of the 115th Squadron, and comments were directed at me personally, things along the line of, "Giora Romm, we're waiting for you."

I certainly couldn't look forward to any sort of bright future in either place, but my desire to settle scores with the Egyptians kept deepening, and I found myself attacking on the Egyptian front daily, from Port Said at the north end of the Canal to armored targets around the city of Suez, near the Bay. The dreams did not return in those days, no matter where I happened to be sleeping. The memories of captivity were put aside, and the only thing on my mind was how to execute my flight missions in the best possible manner. Not because I believed that this or that particular attack I was on the way to carry out would change the face of the war, but because the way to "take care of yourself" in war, as Miriam had urged me when we parted at my parents' house, is to fly correctly and fight correctly, and to avoid professional errors.

In many cases, getting hit in combat is partly due to less than optimal execution by the pilot, and I knew that for many of my comrades, this was essentially the reason why they paid the price, often the ultimate price. I myself had suffered near-fatal blows on two occasions—once in the Six Day War, which put me in Afula Hospital for twenty-four hours before I managed to escape from there, and the second time—when I bailed out of my plane. I'd gone over those two instances in my mind dozens, if not hundreds, of times, and I always knew that, no matter what, there was no one to blame but myself. If I wanted to reduce my chances of getting hit a third time as much as possible, I needed to carry out my combat assignments in the best and most efficient way.

Beyond that, I wanted to execute my flight missions well, with total precision and professionalism, in order to win the absolute respect of the other pilots in my formation, no matter what flight I was leading at that moment. And to be really honest, I wanted to win the respect of all the pilots in my squadron for the method of combat I'd instituted and been overseeing since I was appointed as their commander. On the sixth of October, an extraordinarily tough challenge had been laid at my doorstep, a challenge unlike anything the air force had ever seen before, a nearly unsolvable riddle, and I wanted everyone to see that—in record time, under unbelievable conditions—I had thoroughly cracked it.

On the last day of the war, at five in the afternoon, I attacked targets near the city of Suez. I was with Aharon Ahiaz, Gideon Eli and Miki Barzam. When we finished, I instructed them to return to base without me. I flew a little bit to the east of the Canal and began making my way north, parallel to the Suez Canal. I climbed as high as I could and looked to the west. From this altitude you couldn't tell that a war was raging. The whole area resembled a giant mythical creature lying there quietly, sprawled out in exhaustion. But I didn't climb up there to search for signs of war or to find monsters.

I stared as far into the distance as I could, trying to focus my gaze on the area where I'd dangled from my parachute, limbs shattered, just four years before. At first the Nile Delta appeared as an undifferentiated and indecipherable mass, but with patience I was able to break it down into its constituent parts, mostly by referring to the various water channels within it, and to start identifying different locations. I thought I could make out the city of Mansoura and the surrounding villages, or perhaps I was deluding myself into thinking that's what my eyes were seeing.

At any rate, my thoughts returned to those rural Egyptians in the white *galabiyas*, clutching pickaxes and scythes, from the village of Hajj el-Azz, who surrounded and captured me when I was lying on the ground in the middle of the white cotton field; to the dark-skinned boy who split my brow open with the big rock and almost set off a lynching; and to the young man who wrapped a towel around my bleeding thigh with a well-intentioned but not very effectual tourniquet.

When I reached Port Said at the Canal's northern tip I made a wide turn east to head home, as my thoughts lingered on those indelible figures who had passed through my life during those three months. Was Aziz, my conscientious and determined interrogator, able to provide the Egyptian pilots with good intelligence information before they set out on their missions? Where in this war was the pilot who called himself Anwar, the one who I hoped to meet again one day, and perhaps even befriend? Did he cross eastward over the Suez Canal in his MiG-21 to fight us, or was he back at the command center, dispatching other pilots on their missions? Are Nadia and Aisha still nurses at Al-Maadi Hospital, and if so, have our POWs been among the wounded soldiers they've been tending in the past three weeks? And is Dr. Absalem being more pleasant and patient with those wounded prisoners than he was with me?

Most of all, I want to tell Sami and Othman to be kind and merciful to those POWs who are now in Abbasiya Prison, especially to the prisoner who has been tossed into the last solitary confinement cell, at the end of the hall on the left, the one where the words "They know about you. They'll get you home. It'll be okay." may still be scratched into the wall.

I wondered—with Radio Cairo repeatedly mentioning my name, and my former companions in Egypt aware that I am taking part in the fighting—are they angry at me there in Cairo? And Sayeed—from whom I parted in Qantara, the partially destroyed city on the Canal, before my stretcher was loaded onto the ship, and whose last words to me, "May God be with you," had been echoing in my head since the start of the war—did he understand that I had no choice, that this is our fate, here in the Middle East, until the day that peace arrives?

When I called in for landing, I wanted to identify myself as Tulip Four. Tulip Four, who had just closed a four-year circle of personal experiences that took him to the farthest, most remote edges of human existence, to places that sometimes resembled the corridor that appeared in his dreams, that passage that inexorably narrowed until there was no way to turn back, no way out. But unlike in the dream, even in predicaments that seem utterly hopeless, it is always possible to muster just a little more strength—to save yourself, and eventually to become Peach One, who leads his squadron through this shattering war.

The number of flights had tapered off by now, and when I returned I was the only plane circling to land, which created the sense that quiet was really setting in. I landed and went back to the squadron building. Pedo, the pilot who looked just like Anthony Quinn, whose movies Othman used to act out for me, had landed not long before me. He loved to cook, and he came out to meet me on the steps leading from the parking lot to the porch of the squadron building.

"Commander," he said. "Just drop everything now. Take off your gear and sit and rest. Let me make you the dinner that you deserve, with love from all of us."